W9-BYG-228

Alcohol, Drugs & You

A Young Person's Guide to Avoiding Addiction

Featuring:
The Peanut
vs
The Potato

Marc Treitler with Lianna Treitler

Illustrations by Bennett & Rowena Treitler

Published by DoGood Press

DoGood 9950 Scripps Lake Blvd. #101, San Diego, CA 92131
Press PotatoAllergy.com

Copyright © 2018 by DoGood Press

All rights reserved. No part of this book may be reproduced, stored in a retrieval system, or transmitted by any means, electronic, mechanical, photocopying, recording, or otherwise, without written permission from the author.

Published 2018
First Paperback Edition 2016
Printed in the United States of America

ISBN: 978-0-9974263-2-8
E-ISBN: 978-0-9974263-3-5
Library of Congress Control Number available upon request.

Illustrations by Bennett & Rowena Treitler
Cover and Interior Book Design by Monkey C Media, MonkeyCMedia.com

CONTENTS

Why Should I Read This Book?

This book is written for you—not for your parents, not for your teachers, not for any adult. For *you*. Because as you move towards more and more independence, it is important that you understand the destructiveness of substance abuse and that you are equipped to do what it takes to avoid falling into its trap.

In most families, alcohol is a normal part of entertaining. You see your parents serve drinks to their friends. You might see your mom or dad have a glass of wine or a beer before dinner. For many of you that is just a part of regular life. Others may have parents or grandparents or other relatives who often seem to drink too much. Either way, it is rare for kids to reach adolescence without at least some exposure to adults drinking alcohol.

Familiarity with alcohol, peer pressure, and curiosity lead a lot of kids your age to try alcohol or drugs. What you probably don't realize—what even many adults don't realize—is the potential for these substances to take over your life, to make you dependent upon them forever.

> What is an alcoholic? According to the dictionary, an alcoholic is someone who uses alcohol to excess and becomes addicted to it, to the detriment of their health and well-being.

My children were once where you are now. They did not fully understand what alcohol can do to people. But they had questions and concerns, particularly because one of their parents was an alcoholic. Me. I am that parent. My name is Marc, and I am the father of two wonderful children, Bennett and Lianna, and husband to a wonderful wife, Rowena. I am a successful business person. And I am also an alcoholic. I've been an alcoholic for more than twenty years, but I have been sober (not drinking) for more than eight years now.

Does eight years of sobriety give me the expertise to write a book about addiction and how kids should live their lives? Maybe, maybe not. But I have lived with this addiction for a long time, and I know that there are things I wish I'd been taught as a child, things that might have helped me take a different path. Things that might have kept me from ever activating a disease I will have to work to control for the rest of my life.

For example:

- By the age of 13 most kids are exposed to an opportunity to use alcohol or other addictive substances, and many of them fall prey to trying them.

- More families have members with alcohol-abuse problems than we might think. In fact, according to the National Institute on Alcohol Abuse and Alcoholism, more than thirty percent of Americans have dealt with Alcohol Abuse Disorder.

- It has been estimated that one in twelve Americans has a substance abuse problem requiring treatment.

- Addiction is carried in a family's genes just as eye color, height, or heart disease is. If someone is a drug addict or an alcoholic, the chances are that one of the addict's parents was also an addict.

- Half of all children of addicts become addicts themselves. They follow in the footsteps of their addicted parent, even though they have seen the misery that comes with the disease.

- However, while you might be one of the people born with a predisposition toward addiction, you have a great shot at avoiding the disease because right now you're arming yourself with a very powerful weapon: knowledge.

- You may not know if you have this disease hidden in your genes. Remember that, like blue eye color, this disease can skip generations. So, even if your parents are not alcoholics, your great grandfather may have been and passed along the alcoholic gene to you.

And whether you are someone with addiction in your genes or not, the information in this book will help you avoid falling into the trap of substance abuse.

Because I have been an addict, I see things from an addict's perspective. This means I can honestly speak to you about the downside of substance abuse. It means that when I tell you it is something to avoid, I know *from experience* why this is important.

I have talked to people without addiction in their genes who nevertheless became addicted. I have also met dozens of families that had addiction in their genes, but no one knew about it because it skipped a generation.

One thing these addicts have in common is that none of them was taught, as children, about downside of addiction or about the disease hiding in his or her genes. So, the goal of this book is simple: to make sure that you won't look back in twenty years and say, "I wish someone had just *told* me—"

As with many people who abuse drugs or alcohol, my family's genetic tree includes dozens of addicts and alcoholics—which means that I have addiction in my genes. It also means that my son and daughter have addiction in *their* genes. Lianna and Bennett live with this reality, just as many of you do. But Lianna and I both know that whether you have a family history of substance abuse or not, the prevalence of addiction in today's society puts you at risk. And as many people learn the hard way, it may be in your genes and you don't know it. So, we urge everyone reading this book to act as though it is in their genes.

In this book, you'll hear from Lianna herself; she's written a portion of every chapter. She and I hope that sharing our story will lead you to a strong life free of addiction.

9

Knowledge Is Power

Doctors, politicians, teachers, and addiction specialists have been talking about drug and alcohol addiction for the last hundred years—even at one point legally banning alcohol—and yet the epidemic is getting worse. From one generation to the next, the cycle of addiction continues.

We would love to wave a magic wand and make the disease disappear from society, but we can't. We'd particularly like to make it disappear for those of you with a genetic predisposition towards substance abuse. Maybe in the future someone will be able to alter genes in that way, but for now it's just not possible. But education *is* possible, and it's in your hands right now. This book teaches you facts about the disease and gives you guidance to help you avoid the pitfalls faced by kids today.

When I was growing up, I was ignorant about these facts—as are most kids. In our society, people don't talk much to children about addiction, and they talk even less about inherited addiction. Has a teacher ever cautioned you about substance abuse? Has a relative ever sat you down and told you that addiction runs in your genes? Has your addicted relative ever told you that his or her disease can pass to you in your DNA? Has anyone in your family examined whether your great grandparents or grandparents were addicts? Hopefully you've had these conversations, but most of you probably have not.

The United States spends millions of dollars every year trying to keep kids off of drugs, and that's a fabulous thing. But it's not enough; the numbers tell us that. The fact that thirty percent of Americans have substance abuse problems tells us that. All kids need to know how to avoid the lure of available drugs and alcohol. When children have addiction in their families, they need to know that they are more likely to become addicts themselves, and they need to know the steps they can take to avoid this. And since the genetic link is often unknown, all teens need to face the possibility that they were born with this gene.

Even with millions of dollars spent annually on addiction programs, this is an area that is often missed. I'm making sure that my kids know what I did not know when I was a child, and the person who handed you this book is trying to do the same for you.

This book is an attempt to help you stay substance free. If you have parents or relatives who are addicts, it will help you break the addiction cycle for you in your family. It's too late for me to do that, but it's not too late for you. By reading this book, you will learn secrets that could save you from a lifetime of suffering.

So, let's get started. As the old saying goes: which do you want first, the good news or the bad news?

The Cloud and the Silver Lining

While genetics play a role in whether or not we ever become addicts, so does environment. And in today's environment, drugs and alcohol are not just readily available; their use is also often seen as some sort of status symbol. Kids watch their parents drink with their friends, and it seems cool. Everywhere kids look, someone or something is glamorizing this deadly disease—whether it is rappers talking about drinking cough syrup or actresses glamorizing psychedelic drugs, images of drug and alcohol use probably surround you.

Why Should I Read This Book?

Everyone has the potential to become an addict. The bad news is that if one or both of your parents, or even one of your grandparents or great-grandparents or aunts or uncles has the disease of addiction, you are likely to have it, too. Right now, it is like the potential energy you have probably learned about in science class; it is there, but it is not yet active.

The good news is that if you have alcoholism in your family (even if you don't know it), the disease never has to become active. You can stop it *today*, before it comes to life. And if you do not have the gene, your odds are even better. By following the steps that you will learn in this book, you can make sure that the disease of addiction never affects you.

Think about a sport you like to play, such as baseball. Are you likely to hit a home run if you never practice? No—although it might happen, the odds are against you. Do your chances of hitting a home run increase dramatically if you know how to hold the bat, learn where the pitcher likes to throw the ball, and practice? Yes. Learning about your challenges and how to attack them works with baseball, soccer, school, ... and avoiding the disease of addiction.

Think about how exciting this knowledge is. What other disease can be cured by following a few simple steps throughout your life? You probably know someone who has died of cancer. He or she surely would have paid a million dollars for a cure for that disease. But this disease, alcoholism or addiction, has a simple cure that you will learn in this book—for free.

By the way, in this book we refer to both *addiction* and *alcoholism*, which in reality are the same thing. The disease of addiction uses both drugs and alcohol to hook people. So, when we say either "drugs" or "alcohol," we mean both. That includes both illegal substances, such as heroin, and legal substances you see advertised on TV, such as beer.

If someone gave you this book, it is because they care about you. Whether you are reading it in school, with your parents, or even on your own, take it seriously. If you have one or two parents who are alcoholics or drug addicts, take it even more seriously. Because once we become addicted, even if we find a way to stop, we are addicts for life. Unfortunately, millions of kids your age right now will throw away all of their dreams and aspirations in the name of addiction. You can choose a different path.

If you have addiction in your family, this book is not meant to help cure your parents or to provide counseling about your parents. There are many great books out there about how to deal with addicted family members. This book was written with one goal: to give all kids real insight into why and how to avoid addiction and to provide those with addiction in their genes a fighting chance to live a normal life.

The simple facts and advice we present give you a leg up when it comes to avoiding addiction. Unfortunately— even in today's medically advanced world—the most common treatment for addiction for kids is prevention through scare tactics, where you are told to "just say no." This rarely works for kids like you, because the real danger to you of taking that first drug or first drink is not known; and remember, if you have addiction in your family, that danger is multiplied. The other most common treatment is rehabilitation, but that comes years after addiction begins. What you need *now*, at your age, is a much better treatment: knowledge.

You can avoid addiction. You just need the knowledge to do so. We want to help. Father and daughter, we're here for you, telling you the things we wish someone had told us.

So, get ready; this book was written for you.

As I finished this chapter and sat staring at my computer, my mind drifted to a day many years ago, when my children were off to the first day of school together—Bennett to kindergarten and Lianna to second grade. They had been preparing for this day for months. You could smell the excitement in the air, and the anticipation had kept them up most of the night.

My wife diligently prepared all their supplies, and at 7:00 a.m. sharp our SUV left the driveway with two excited kids, one proud mother, and ... an empty passenger seat. You see, although my family was and is the most important thing in the world to me, the night before the big day arrived, my disease had won again. I was drunk and alone—and slept through that magnificent morning. In fact, on most school days during my children's elementary years I was missing, hungover, and ashamed.

Those were the days when I missed out on my children's lives. Those were the days when I was an absent father. Those were the days that were filled with regret. Those were the days that I must never forget. Those are the days of my disease.

What Is an Addict?

An addict is a person who has a disease that makes it almost impossible to stop using drugs or drinking alcohol on his or her own. If your mom cannot stop using drugs, then she has the disease of addiction. If your father drinks beer every night, he might have the disease of alcoholism, which is also a type of addiction.

Experts say that addicts, unlike non-addicts, are "allergic" to drugs and alcohol. This "allergy" makes it almost impossible for an addict to stop drinking or using drugs once he or she has started. And while those with addiction in their family have a much greater chance of it happening to them, the truth is that anyone can develop an addiction.

The addict's brain reacts differently to certain substances than a non-addict's brain does. Fancy scientific tests developed in the last few decades have given doctors the ability to actually watch how a person's brain reacts to drugs and alcohol. These machines produce images showing that an addict's brain behaves differently after he or she drinks a single beer than a non-addict's brain does. It's like what would happen to a friend of yours who has a peanut allergy: she starts to swell up after eating a single peanut, while you have no reaction at all. The addict's brain says, "Have another drink!" while the non-addict's brain says, "Let's go home."

Remember, we're talking about a *disease*. Your addicted mom or dad or aunt or uncle or grandparent or cousin isn't choosing drugs over you. He or she loves you but

You look tasty.

HELP!

NOOO!

suffers from a disease that is very hard to overcome once it becomes active. Much of the crazy or mean behavior you see from him or her is a product of the disease itself, not your loved one. Millions of parents have this disease, and almost all of them want to stop using drugs and become a better father or mother—but the disease is powerful, and it often wins.

Blaming and Curing

Most importantly, if you have a parent who is an addict or an alcoholic, you need to remember that your parent's addiction is not your fault. If you get into a fight with your mom and afterward she gets drunk, that's not your fault. She has a disease. If you fight with your sister and then your dad gets angry and drunk, that's not your fault. He has a disease. If your mom divorces your dad because he's angry and drunk all the time, that's not your fault either. Remember: no matter how crazy or selfish their behavior may seem to you, addicts are not choosing drugs over you; their disease is making the choice. Nothing you do is *ever* the cause of someone else's addictive behavior.

On the other hand, you're also not the cure for that addictive behavior. In fact, once the disease of addiction has been activated, it can never be cured like other diseases can. It can only be controlled. Addiction will always stay with the addict, waiting for a chance to re-appear. Addicts have to work the rest of their lives to keep the now-activated disease under control. You will see successful recovering alcoholics, for example, attending AA meetings for the rest of their lives. And although AA meetings are often very enjoyable to attend, every one of the people sitting in that room would have chosen, if he or she had known, not to have turned the disease on in the first place so many years ago.

> Children of an alcoholic are up to eight times more likely to become alcoholics than are the children of a non-alcoholic.

So, why can one person have a couple of beers and go home, but an addict cannot? Simply stated, it's because an addict's brain is not built for it. This is a painful fact learned by millions of people who developed the disease of addiction. And, again, almost all experts agree that addicts do not get cured. They can never again use alcohol or drugs occasionally or casually, as other people can.

Unfortunately for you, the disease of addiction has been proven over and over to be inherited from a parent or a grandparent (it can skip a generation). So if your mother, father, aunt, uncle, grandparent, or great grandparent is or was an alcoholic or drug addict, you very likely carry the same predisposition for the disease. In fact, studies have shown that children of an alcoholic are up to eight times more likely to become alcoholics than are the children of a non-alcoholic. Those are not good odds, and that percentage is reflected throughout our society.

Switch On, Switch Off

On the other hand, experts also agree that the disease of addiction never *has* to show itself in your life. If a person simply avoids alcohol and addictive narcotics (illegal or legal), the disease stays hidden, inactive, in his or her DNA.

What you also have to know is that while a person with addiction in their family is up to eight times more likely to be susceptible to addiction, even if you do not have addiction in your family, you can become an addict. Environment, personality, and so many other factors can play a role in making drugs and alcohol dangerous for you.

This means you have two choices: (1) use drugs or alcohol and potentially become an addict, or (2) never use alcohol or drugs, and keep the disease away.

I sure could have used this knowledge in high school! Instead, it took me twenty years to learn the facts listed here—twenty years of battling a disease I didn't understand, and in the process almost losing my family.

When I finally went through a twenty-eight-day program at a rehab facility (where addicts go to "rehabilitate," or get better), one thought kept going through my mind: "I wish I'd known this when I was young." What if, during my college years, I'd been told that I had a fatal disease and couldn't drink alcohol like a normal college student (which, at my school, meant drinking several times a week)? What if I'd known that this disease was easy to avoid? And what about the rest of my family? What if my sister and cousins had been informed that youthful experimentation with drugs would lead them into a lifelong struggle with addiction?

Why didn't my parents talk to me about the addiction in my family? Maybe they thought I'd learn about the subject in school. Maybe they didn't know, themselves, that addiction descends from one generation to the next. Maybe they were ashamed, or simply didn't know what to say.

Whatever the reason, this situation occurs all the time, in families all over the world. The dangers associated with drugs and alcohol are not discussed. Addiction is not talked about with those who need it the most—children with addiction in their families, built into the cells of their own bodies. And without this knowledge, the cycle of addiction just keeps repeating—from grandparent to parent, parent to child.

It bears repeating: non-addicts can drink alcohol and not become alcoholics. People with alcoholism in their genes, however, probably do not have this luxury. One drink too many in high school or college could turn you into an alcoholic forever.

You might be thinking, "It's not fair. Why me?" Well, we're all given gifts and challenges when we're born. A child starving in Africa probably wouldn't feel sorry for you and your addictive genes. A child who needs a wheelchair would probably trade places with you, if you are not physically challenged yourself. A kid living in an orphanage would probably trade places with a kid like you living in a nice house, even if you do have addiction in your genes.

But don't forget that good news/bad news thing. It's very good news that your condition might never turn into a full-blown disease. You have the control, and now you have the knowledge.

Thoughts from Lianna

My name is Lianna. I'm a teenager, and I decided that this is an important subject for kids in a tough situation. This book is meant to help you avoid addiction. I hope you find all of this information and my "expert opinion" helpful. I have experienced addiction up close and fortunately learned from my dad's disease. I know better than to give in to the villainous power of drugs and alcohol, because I have the knowledge revealed in this book.

To me, an alcoholic is someone who is addicted to bad things. Alcoholism has the same symptoms as drug addiction, but usually when people talk about an alcoholic they mean someone who is addicted to beer, wine, and liquor. When people talk about a drug addict, they mean the person is addicted to drugs—even medical drugs prescribed by a doctor.

You might not be sure that your mom or dad has a disease until after you read this book, but it is very important to know if he or she does. There are ways to help him or her and yourself. It might be scary to face the truth, but hopefully this book will be comforting to you. In my family, there are a lot of people with this specific disease, and they couldn't help themselves because they didn't know about their propensity for addiction until after they were addicted. With this book, you will be able to help yourself. It's good to have this knowledge, especially if you, like me, have addiction in your genes.

To prepare you for the rest of this book, I have two questions:
1. Does one of your relatives do things that you know are wrong?
2. Does he or she say things that hurt your feelings or make you feel bad about yourself?

If these things are happening to you, you will learn how to defend yourself by reading this book. If a relative is doing bad things in front of you, don't follow his or her example, and don't *ever* believe that you are to blame.

I have always found faith to be an important part of me, and I believe it has helped both my father and me throughout our lives. Thinking about a God who loves unconditionally has allowed me to get rid of any stress and fear that I experience.

During the years of my dad's drinking, my parents would often fight. I would end up shutting myself in my room trying to avoid the yelling and pounding on the walls. And although all parents fight, some of these late-night arguments would get louder and louder by the minute. The words they screamed at each other would replay for hours in my head, and the sounds would echo in my mind until I could fall asleep. In those desperate times, I would often pray that my parents would find happiness and that God would blanket our house with His care and make the fighting stop.

At the time, I did not know that I was really praying for my dad to find sobriety and faith in God for himself. Even though it took time, I truly believe that God heard my prayers. You will find devotional messages in each chapter of this book to help get you thinking and enlighten you if you are unhappy with what you learned in the previous sections. I picked each text directly from the Bible. I go to a Catholic school, and I believe that God is a huge part of my dad's recovery. I really hope that you can connect with each devotion in your own way and relate to the messages from every passage. Even if you are not Catholic, try to uncover the meaning of each Scripture.

Devotional Message

"I cried unto the Lord with my voice; with my voice unto the Lord did I make my supplication. I poured out my complaint before him; I shewed before him my trouble. When my spirit was overwhelmed within me, then thou knewest my path." —Psalm 142:1–3a

Many people complain to and blame God for the presence of addiction in their lives. Just remember, God has a plan for all of us. It's okay if you feel angry or overwhelmed by the trouble going on in your life, but God knows what He's doing. Your whole family can learn from the addiction. Try to turn to the bright side of your situation, and God will be there to talk to you through prayer.

Like the devotional message says, you might be tempted to place blame for your unhappiness or trouble on someone else, but there is always a path laid out for you. Take the time to realize that everything is going to be okay; God is continuously watching over you.

CHAPTER
3

Drugs and The Legalization Trend

Before we discuss drugs in detail, we have to answer one fundamental question. For addiction, are drugs different than alcohol? No.

No, no, no, no, no. An alcoholic dad is no different from a drug addict living on the street. A woman hiding bottles of vodka is no different from a man concealing his cocaine. Millions of addicts, including me, fall into the trap of pointing at addicts who are worse off than themselves in order to excuse their own behavior. For years, I justified my alcoholism by saying, "Well, I never do drugs." Yet I ended up in the same rehab as heroin addicts.

I have known addicts who take only pills prescribed by doctors and never drink alcohol. I've known addicts

who only smoke marijuana; they avoid beer. Yet they all ended up in the same place.

The brain of an addict does not care whether drugs or alcohol are entering the addict's system. To your brain, alcohol is a drug and drugs are alcohol.

An alcoholic can easily transfer his addiction to heroin because his brain treats both substances the same way. To your brain, alcohol is a drug and drugs are alcohol. So, if your mom is taking too many pain pills or your dad is drinking too many beers, they might both be addicted.

Tough Questions

Becoming addicted to drugs, alcohol, or both is a complex and often misunderstood process, and the last thing we want to do is confuse you. So here are some common questions that are often answered incorrectly; knowing the truth might help you understand:

1. If your dad uses drugs, can he safely drink alcohol?

   No. The addict's brain reacts the same way to drugs and alcohol.

2. If your mom stops using drugs, can she safely drink alcohol?

   No. This may lead her back to drugs, and using any drugs or alcohol is what the disease wants.

3. Can an alcoholic ever drink like a normal person?

   No. If your dad is an alcoholic, he shouldn't ever drink again.

4. Are some drugs safe?

   Not for an addict. Even laughing gas at a dentist's office can be dangerous for an addict.

5. How do I know what to avoid?

   This book and many other resources can help you. Basically, avoid any substance that alters your mind. Here's a good list to start with:

- Beer

  Even "non-alcoholic" beer contains small amounts of alcohol and should be avoided.

- Wine

  Any and all types of wine should be avoided.

- Liquor

  Vodka, tequila, rum, gin, and whiskey are all common types of liquor.

- Marijuana

- Crack Molly, MDA

- Cocaine

- Opiates

  Many times, opiates are obtained from a doctor, but that fact does not mean that they are safe. We devote an entire chapter to opiates because so many people become addicted to pain pills. These pills go by many names, including Vicodin, morphine, and OxyContin.

- Heroin

- Benzos

  These pills, which are used to help with anxiety in normal people, are extremely dangerous to addicts.

- Valium

- Crystal Meth

- "Bath salts" or other synthetic drugs
  These dangerous new products are meant to imitate the effects of other drugs, are not safe, and can be deadly to an addict.

What makes many of these substances so dangerous is that addicts often become addicted to them after trying them only once. Yes, *once.* Thousands of heroin addicts will tell you that they knew they could not stop using heroin the very first time they used it.

Does addiction happen to a normal person? Sometimes. Can it happen to anyone who has addictive genes? Yes. So, if you have addiction in your family, and if your friends in high school are passing around drugs, you need to remember that although *they* might be able to use it this one time and never again, *your* single use could activate your addiction gene, and your entire life might be altered. And as thousands of kids realize every year, addiction may be hidden in your genes, sent from family members generations ago. When those friends pressure you, the safe approach is to act as though you do have a predisposition. Be smart and say no.

Choose Your Poison . . . and It's All Poison

For whatever reason, I was never into drugs. In fact, the only times I tried a drug (marijuana), I hated it! It terrified me. I found myself blacking out every two to three minutes for hours and praying for the horror to end. This handful of experiences was enough to keep me away from drugs forever.

> ... whether a person's drug of choice is heroin or beer, anyone who is unable to stop using the substance is an addict.

What I did not know at the time was that my dreadful reaction to marijuana was a blessing in disguise, because battling alcohol was hard enough. If I had also used drugs, who knows where I would have ended up? Most likely, I wouldn't be here, writing this book.

What is clear to me, as it is to every expert in the field of addiction, is that whether a person's drug of choice is heroin or beer, anyone who is unable to stop using the substance is an addict.

The things I know about drugs I've learned from other addicts, including my siblings, aunts, uncles, and cousins. I'll share a few of their tragic stories, which have devastated our family. I believe that if these talented individuals had known the threat of lifelong addiction that can result from youthful drug experimentation, they probably would have made different choices and led totally different lives. None of these people would have intentionally turned down a road that led to a life of drugs and misery. If they'd known that simply avoiding these drugs in high school would have saved them, they might have done so.

How many people would *deliberately* choose a pill from a friend at a party over a life that could have been full of joy and adventure? How many would prefer to live in misery, rehab, and jail rather than simply telling a friend in high school "No"?

My sister, Beth Treitler, was born a happy, caring, and brilliant child with all the gifts needed to live a great life. She and I were raised by caring parents and had all the material things we needed. Beth was a lovely girl, gifted in school, who excelled at everything she tried. She also cared about others; she was that girl in class who would always take home injured birds or cats to heal.

Unfortunately, during high school she started experimenting with drugs. She also battled mental illnesses. Now, can some kids experiment with drugs in high school and never do them again? Sure—unless, like Beth, they have addiction in their genes. Then it's a bad bet.

Beth spent twenty years in misery, fighting her addiction to drugs and alcohol, as well as severe mental illness. She was in and out of mental hospitals, and she once spent ninety days in a rehab facility before she got kicked out. For her, every day was a battle, and this caring, talented individual became engulfed by addiction and mental disorders.

My cousin, whom I will call Jay, was also a talented individual, but he was born into a life of drugs and alcohol. I remember him using drugs in front of me on a vacation to California at the age of twelve. Today, Jay's life is spent in and out of rehabs, jails, and other institutions. He is addicted to heroin, often lives on the streets, and struggles to provide basic necessities for his daughter. He has been a slave to drugs for at least twenty years, and he hates it. He owns no cars and no homes, and he cannot hold a job. His ability to be a good father and son was destroyed by addiction.

Jay's brother—let's call him Sam—was fortunate enough to avoid drugs and alcohol in high school. He is now happily married and working for a great Internet company in Silicon Valley. He owns a home and two cars and has many happy days.

Jay has no happy days.

Sam and Jay are brothers. They had the same talents and potential; they grew up in the same house with the same parents and in the same neighborhood. So how did one man become a lifelong heroin addict and the other a successful computer programmer with a nice house, cars, and family? I believe the answer is clear: one started using drugs in junior high school, and the other never started at all. So, although they both carry genes for addiction (their father to this day battles with massive addiction issues), one avoided turning on those genes, and the other ensured that it happened.

Remember, many people *do* experiment with drugs at a young age and later grow out of it. My best advice to you all would be to *never* do so, but not all of you will follow that advice. However, for the children of addicts this advice is imperative; you are at far greater risk than other kids. Our brains are more sensitive to drugs than the brains of normal people. We cannot simply turn off our craving for drugs or alcohol once our brains have been exposed to them. And since there is no way for you to know if you have addiction in your genes, the safe approach is to act as though you do.

Several years ago, my addicted cousin visited my family in San Diego. At that point in his life, he had been drug free for a year and was actively participating in recovery programs such as Narcotics Anonymous. He told me how much better his life was sober, and how he could be a father to his fourteen-year-old daughter. We went together to a Narcotics Anonymous meeting. He knew all of the prayers and sayings by heart and was obviously taking his recovery seriously. At the end of his visit, as we said goodbye, I was very proud of him.

Sadly, a few months later I heard he had relapsed and was again using heroin on a daily basis. As I write this, I'm scared I will never see him again. I wish I could go back in time to when we were twelve years old and playing in the canyon, and tell him that if he ever started using drugs he would ruin his life forever.

A question for you: *which brother do you want to be?*

As this book is about to go to print, our country is in the midst of a troubling trend of legalizing marijuana. On January 1, 2018 California became the latest state to make recreational use of marijuana legal. California joins states such as Oregon, Washington, Colorado and Nevada to allow adults to use marijuana in virtually the same manner alcohol is used.

While promoting our first book on radio and TV stations, I am often asked if this trend is a good idea. I am asked, "Is marijuana a "gateway" drug?", "Do you agree with legalizing marijuana," and "Will making it legal make kids more likely to use it."

My answer, which is the correct one when discussing addiction, is that making marijuana legal is a horrible idea for our children and the fight against addiction.

Let me explain why with a few different approaches, the first being with a few statistics. Before that, however, we must understand that there is a massive amount of power and wealth behind this legalization effort. This means that studies will be performed (and funded by the industry) that demonstrate how great marijuana legalization is for our society. On any given talk show, you will find industry paid "experts" presenting mountains of scientific studies supporting the claim that marijuana is not a gateway drug and legalization benefits society. When you see these studies, think about the billion-dollar company that is completely dependent on its product becoming legal.

The industry is a powerful one and is only growing. And it has an agenda.

According to Arcview Market Research's 2017 report, legal sales of marijuana are expected to surpass $22 billion by 2020. To put that in perspective, the total sales of all suntan products (lotion, spray, aftercare balm) in 2016 was only $1.6 billion. Imagine if the government tried to make suntan products illegal and the fight those companies would put up. That is exactly what we are seeing in reverse—a massive industry pushing to legalize its sole product to increase its own profits.

Now for a few legitimate statistics that you will not see on any pro-legalization website:

- In Colorado, the Colorado Children's Hospital saw a 400% increase in marijuana-intoxicated teenagers after legalization.

- The US Government, via its National Survey on Drug Use and Health in 2013 found that people who are addicted to marijuana are 300% more likely to become addicted to heroin than those not addicted to marijuana.

- Yale researchers found that individuals who used marijuana in the past were 250% more likely to abuse prescription pills than those who had not used marijuana.

I could provide 50 more examples of statistics showing the damaging effects of marijuana and its legalization, but you get the idea.

Now let's look at this issue with some common sense. Start by asking yourself why do people follow laws? Why do people go 65 instead of 100 on an empty freeway? Why do people often wait for a walk sign at a deserted intersection? Why do drivers make sure they have an updated registration sticker on their car? Are these laws followed because we think the act itself is dangerous? Or are we simply trying to avoid getting in trouble? The answer is clear; people stay near the speed limit on freeways because they do not want a ticket. If I was guaranteed that there would be no police officers on a deserted freeway tonight I, along with most adults, would certainly be traveling near 100mph. Only the thought of another ticket keeps us from pushing the limits.

Laws are often purely deterrents; they are enacted to deter people from taking certain actions, like speeding. Now deterrents do not work for everyone. Just look around you next time you are on a freeway. But the vast majority of drivers do abide by the speed limit because the law says so.

So, what would happen if speed limits were removed? As I have personally seen in Germany (where most freeways have no speed limits) it is the norm to go over 100mph. So, what happens when the fear of the law is taken away and marijuana is legalized? Obviously, more people will use it. The deterrent is gone, and those people that avoided using marijuana for fear of the law will now use it. Add easy access with stores in most mini-malls, and use escalates even further. Its common sense.

I have spent the last 30 years of my life in, and researching, addiction. I can tell you a few things about marijuana. First, it is absolutely addictive. Anyone saying it is not has an agenda to legalize it or is in denial. I have seen hundreds of people addicted to marijuana, inside and outside of rehabs. To me this is not even debatable.

Second, I call marijuana the ambition-killer in people. I have seen it since the 1980s when I was in high school. Once brilliant, ambitious and talented people that start smoking marijuana slowly lose their drive and ambition and prefer to "get high" and "chill out." Look around your daily lives at the people who are heavy marijuana users. Are those the people making the most out of school, life, and their own potential?

Or are those the people most likely to watch movies all weekend on the couch.

Finally, let me provide an analogy that adults reading this book can understand. Marijuana has a few similarities with alcohol, one being that tolerances are built up over time for heavy users. The alcoholics and marijuana addicts must use more and more of the substance to achieve the same results over time. For the alcoholic, this means that more and more alcohol must be consumed over time. So, a beer drinker that has six beers a day early on may have to consume twelve beers daily a few years into his alcoholism. Now the reality is drinking twelve beers is difficult physically; it is a lot of liquid. So almost inevitably, alcoholics move from beer to vodka. Drinking 12 ounces of vodka is much easier to manage than 144 ounces of beer.

The switch from beer to vodka for an alcoholic is very similar to why marijuana addicts find themselves trying opiates or other drugs. Smoking ten joints a day to get high enough simply becomes too difficult. Eventually the user looks for something, like an opiate pill to get him a quicker high.

When adults go to a bar with a big group of people, the group usually starts off drinking individual beers, wine, and mixed drinks. Then a few hours pass and what happens? Someone calls out for shots. This person, and others, are looking for a quicker method to get drunk. Drinking individual beers takes too long and gets too boring. I would estimate that on the hundreds of occasions in my life where I was with a large group at a bar, this pattern of moving to shots occurred 90% of the time. The same pattern happens with groups of people together using marijuana; it is human nature. After a few hours someone is going to whip out pills or other drugs to pick up the pace of the party and speed up the high. In social scenes, beer turns to shots and marijuana turns to pills or cocaine.

To summarize my thoughts on the legalization movement; marijuana is an addictive gateway drug that sucks ambition out of people. The paid spokespeople for the billion-dollar marijuana companies will not tell you this, but I will. Legalization is a terrible trend that is going to produce millions of more drug addicts in our country. That makes the message in this book even more important for our teens and pre-teens. Addiction and alcoholism has a 100% cure rate if we never start using, whether it is illegal or legal.

Thoughts from Lianna

Drugs and alcohol aren't very different from each other. In no way are either drugs or alcohol safe to use, not even if you're an adult. Drugs and alcohol can do serious harm to anyone who consumes them. With alcoholic genes already implanted in your genetic makeup, you (and I!) have to stay away from both.

Think about the harmful effects of both drugs and alcohol. Here is some space to lay down your thoughts:

Devotional Message

"I guide you in the way of wisdom and lead you along straight paths. When you run you will not stumble."
—Proverbs 4:11–12a

God tries His best to guide us in the right direction. Even though people don't always make the right decisions, think about what you're doing and consider the consequences of every decision you make. It's okay to make mistakes, but you should work to do the right thing. God wants you to be happy and successful. Try your best to do what He asks of you, even when it's hard.

Once your family member stops drinking and doing drugs, trust in God that he or she will not start using drugs and alcohol again. God will do everything in His power to guide your family member to stay away from both. Like I said, He wishes the best for you always; know that God will guide and protect you.

CHAPTER

4

How Can I Tell?

Many of you have never had a reason to wonder whether or not anyone in your family is addicted to alcohol or drugs. Others might wonder if your mom, dad, or other family member is an addict. There is no physical test, like testing for blood type. But because addiction is such a common problem, a variety of yes or no questions have been developed to help people determine if they—or someone they love—have a problem with drugs or alcohol. If you're wondering if a member of your family is addicted, here are some simple questions to ask yourself:

1. Do your parents fight about the amount of alcohol or drugs one or both of them use?

2. Does either of your parents drink alcohol or use drugs every day?

3. Has either of your parents been arrested for driving under the influence (also called a DUI) of alcohol or drugs?

4. Has your mom or dad lost a job because of drug or alcohol use?

5. Does your parent's drinking or drug use result in odd or bizarre behavior?

Consider asking the person who gave you this book why he or she gave it to you. Does he or she believe someone in your family might be addicted to drugs or alcohol?

Identifying an addict in your family tree will help you understand the disease you may face.

> ... alcohol also often seems to play a big role in families where addiction is not the norm.

For me, the addicts in the family tree are easy to spot. My mom has brothers, sisters, and nephews who are full-blown drug addicts or alcoholics. They've spent years in and out of jail and rehab and struggled to find and keep places to live. The addiction on my mom's side of the family has never been a secret.

But alcohol also often seems to play a big role in families where addiction is not the norm. My dad's side is a different story from my mom's. Everyone on that side drinks a lot, but they've been able to hold down jobs and maintain the appearance of being normal. In fact, drinking stories are part of our family lore; tales of who drank what at certain events, and what silly things were done at these parties, have always been shared with a sense of pride at family get-togethers. Many families glorify the use of alcohol, even if there's an addict or two in the clan. Most likely, you've been to weddings or other family events where all of the adults were drinking alcohol.

Growing up, I thought alcohol use was normal—part of a well-functioning family. However, a more in-depth analysis of events has made me aware of the arrests, constant fights with spouses, and other things that look a lot like signs of addiction.

So my family had a dangerous mix of addiction—heavy drinkers on my dad's side and drug addicts on my mom's. What happens when you mix drug addicts and heavy drinkers? Well, you get two children in rehab— one an alcoholic (me) and one addicted to both drugs and alcohol (my sister).

Nature or Nurture?

Did I have a chance to avoid all this when I was growing up? Was my sister's twenty-year battle with alcohol and drugs preventable, or was her future life in and out of rehabs and mental institutions carved in stone long before she even tried drugs? Did I have a chance to avoid the disease instead of spending my college years hanging out with fraternity buddies who drank? I'll never know the answers to these questions. But I do know that I was never taught the things contained in this book—nor was my sister, nor any other addict I have spoken with. No one ever told us that experimenting with drugs in high school, or heavy drinking in college, might turn our young, healthy brains into addicted brains—permanently. I was never told that one drink or a single hit of a drug could activate my hidden disease forever; I never knew that recreational drinking could be problematic. I thought everyone in college drank, and that drunks were people who lived on the streets.

Too often addiction is not something that is discussed. If it exists in a family, it is considered embarrassing. If it does not, it is considered unimportant. But the reality is, with drugs and alcohol as available as they are these days and with their use considered almost 'normal,' a conversation about the dangers inherent to them is absolutely necessary. The average American child begins drinking in middle school. Shouldn't the conversation about the danger of drinking take place by then?

Also, in my research, I discovered that addict families are less likely to discuss serious issues than non-addict families are. Addict families tend to bottle up emotions and often treat family issues with a "better off not spoken about" attitude.

Thoughts from Lianna

Think: has one of your family members seemed to change lately? Is he or she acting differently? More aggressive than usual? Is he or she yelling at you, throwing or hitting things, or even pushing you?

Think again: are *you* getting more aggressive lately? If so, it could be because you're in an aggressive environment. On the other hand, you might have become passive in all your words or actions—meaning that you are not as active or determined. These changes could happen because you're afraid someone might start yelling or getting angry with you. It's okay to be scared, but you should still be yourself.

You might notice your parents fighting more often. If that happens, remember, it's not because they don't love each other anymore; it's because the addicted parent is harder to agree with because he or she isn't thinking straight due to the influence of drugs or alcohol. Addiction can cause a family member to argue more or make bad decisions more often. Addicts also might not be as energetic or interactive as they used to be. If your parents or relatives take drugs or drink too much, the next morning they are basically sick, so they might not even want to get out of bed.

If you're experiencing any of these things, you should talk to a trusted adult. Remember, this isn't tattling or being mean; telling the truth is always for the better. Your courage will help you, your parent(s), and everyone around you. While your parent is suffering from this disease, it's likely everyone else finds him or her hard to deal with too.

Even though your parent(s) might be changing, it is not their intention to hurt you or anybody else. It is simply a part of addiction.

Here's a space to write some things that you've observed about your family member. Think about the signs of addiction:

Devotional Message

"Take notice, you senseless ones among the people; you fools, when will you become wise?" —Psalm 94:8

Take the time to look for signs, and be aware of changes in your daily environment. Because addiction can be hard to recognize, you need to become wise and empower yourself to spot signs of the disease.

CHAPTER

5

Is He Changing?

Addiction is a progressive disease. In other words, over time it gets worse, not better. Alcoholics do not "grow out of it." Heroin addicts do not "get better over the years."

Because of this downward spiral, a dad in his first year of alcoholism is much different from a dad in his fifteenth year. A mother in her first year of addiction to prescription pills is much different from a mother in her tenth year of addiction.

An adolescent—someone like you—moving into addiction is not who or what she will be by the time she finishes college—if she ever does finish school.

Most experts believe that there are four stages of alcoholism and other addictions. The following are quick summaries of those stages. The most important thing for you to remember is that if you follow the steps you learn in this book, *you* do not have to enter any of these stages!

Experimentation/Adaptive Stage

People begin to use drugs regularly and experiment with different substances. They drink more than others when they do drink. They use drugs or alcohol as a regular way to cope with life's problems rather than actually dealing with those problems. This cycle most often begins in the teenage years, but it can begin earlier.

Dependence

People feel a physical and mental need to drink or use drugs. Others start to notice that they use drugs or drinks more than other people do. Physically, bad things happen to them more regularly, such as being sick all day after a night of drinking or using drugs, daily stomach problems, or high blood pressure.

People in this stage try to plan their social events around drugs/alcohol. One example is a dad who always takes his kids out to eat, or to have fun, at a place where alcohol is sold. This is not difficult in our society. Think about all the fun places that serve beer: Sea World, Chuck E. Cheese, Dave & Buster's, Disneyland. For non-addicts, the ability to buy beer at family fun zones might be fine, but for an addict at this stage, having a drink is more than a pleasure; it's a necessity.

A young person moving into addiction might choose to hang out with other kids at whose homes alcohol is readily available or who bring drugs and alcohol to school.

When you see homeless people living on the street, many of them are in this last stage of addiction; their lives revolve around drugs, and they cannot stay sober enough to hold a job. People in this stage often suffer permanent damage to parts of their body, such as their livers, stomachs, lungs, and brains.

Progression

This is the stage where people lose control of their urges more and more frequently. Often, when they try to have one or two beers, they end up having fifteen. Parents may begin to neglect their children; there is always some excuse, it seems, for the parents not to attend their kids' school or sports functions. Using drugs or drinking alcohol becomes the most important thing in the person's life; the disease has taken over. It is very common in this stage for a person to lose his or her job, get arrested, or get divorced. This is also a common stage in which the addict tries to quit—but can rarely do so without help.

For young people, it may hamper their ability to attend school. Their parents might buy the excuse of a stomach bug or the flu at first, but soon it begins to be obvious that something is wrong.

Final Stage

This is often known as the "conclusion" stage, because people who are in this stage and have no help almost always end up going to jail, living in a mental institution, or dying. They cannot function without the daily consumption of their drug of choice. They use drugs or drink almost all day—from the moment they wake up until they fall asleep (the person may often become unconscious, or pass out, instead of falling asleep normally). A person in this stage can rarely maintain a job or a marriage, or function as a parent. When you see homeless people living on the street, many of them are in this last stage of addiction; their lives revolve around drugs, and they cannot stay sober enough to hold a job. People in this stage often suffer permanent damage to parts of their body, such as their livers, stomachs, lungs, and brains.

20/20 Vision

The four stages listed here progress in this order for almost every addict in the world. A true addict has little hope of staying in one stage rather than moving on to the next. Millions of addicts have tried to halt the progression, but almost all have failed. If an addict in Stage One doesn't get help, he or she will end up in Stage Four.

People in Stage Four might look strange to you, but don't forget that they started out as normal kids your age—not using drugs, not drinking alcohol, not living on the streets. Although they might have experienced tragedies in their lives, most of them could have avoided the streets if they had never started using drugs or alcohol.

If this information scares you a bit, that's normal and okay. The life of an addict is not fun, and without help addicts almost always end up in misery that affects not only them but everyone they know. But remember, this is a disease that can have a 100 percent prevention rate. Just follow what you learn in this book, and you will avoid addiction. For those of you predisposed to addiction, it will stay hidden in your genes for the rest of your life.

Imagine asking a homeless drug addict, "If you could go back in time, would you turn down the first drug someone gave you in high school?" Imagine asking a father who has lost custody of his kids due to his alcoholism, and now spends all day drinking, "Would you like to go back in time and refuse that first beer at a football game?" You might have heard the phrase "Hindsight is 20/20," meaning it is easy to see *now* what you should have done in the past. We want to provide you with the ability to make that choice *now* instead of looking back in twenty years, full of regrets.

If an addict never enters Stage One, there is nothing to progress from, and Stage Four will never come.

When I was in the active phase of my disease, it was hard for me to recognize the fact that I was getting worse every year. Addiction has ways of hiding reality from us. Now, looking back, it is clear that my disease worsened just as described here. Year after year, it spiraled downward, but thankfully I was able to stop (with professional help) before I reached the final stage. If I had made it to that stage, I certainly would have died.

Now, I don't want this book to be about the progression of my disease; it's about how *you* can avoid the disease entirely. Still, I think a quick snapshot of the stages of my disease will help you understand how easily you can go from "one innocent drink" to full-blown addiction:

High School

I was not much of a drinker or a drug user in high school. This isn't the case with most addicts, who often start their addictions in their teens. But at that time, I was focused on school and sports and wasn't in the partying crowd. My drinking was limited to two or three occasions a year.

As I described earlier, I did try marijuana a few times, but it had a terrifying effect on me—which was a blessing, because I was never tempted to try drugs again. I thank God for this all the time. That negative reaction to marijuana was probably the only thing that stopped me from a lifelong battle with drugs as well as alcohol.

> ... once the addiction gene is switched on, it never gets switched off.

At that point, I had no idea that I suffered from the disease of addiction. If I had stopped drinking entirely then, I never would have become an alcoholic.

But that was not how things worked out.

College

In college, I made up for the drinking I didn't do in high school. Unfortunately, for an addict, college often presents the perfect opportunity to feed the disease. Alcohol and drugs are everywhere. I had friends and a roommate who liked to drink as much as I did. (The roommate is still a good friend of mine—and is also an addict who has been to rehab.) From the moment I started college, I drank nightly. Yes, *nightly*. This didn't seem abnormal to me, and my parents were not around to question it. Thus, I found the perfect formula for alcohol abuse: alcohol was all around me, and I had no supervision.

Let me say that again: once the addiction gene is switched on, it never gets switched off.

Before long, I joined a fraternity where almost every member drank regularly. As a result, my nightly drinking habit was never questioned—especially because I wasn't even one of the biggest drinkers in my fraternity. In fact, years later when I entered rehab, my frat brothers were shocked; I was not someone they pictured ever being in rehab. Of course, hiding the disease is a common trait of addicts, so the fact that no one knew how much I really drank is typical.

In my crowd, nightly drinking was so normal that I had no idea I was feeding a disease. I just thought it was part of a normal college experience. My grades were fine, and soon I was off to law school. Things seemed great. However, after four years of nightly drinking, the truth is this: I was probably already an active alcoholic.

Law School

This was when I turned from being a "big drinker" into what was clearly an alcoholic. The disease works that way: once you make that turn, you can never go back ... and you don't even realize you're making a turn. But once the addiction gene is switched on, it never gets switched off.

Let me say that again: *once the addiction gene is switched on, it never gets switched off.* And while it is more common for someone with addiction in their family to have the gene turned on, it really can happen to anyone. There are plenty of addicts and alcoholics out there without a family history to point to or who had the addiction in their genes and didn't know it.

So, sometime during those years of nightly drinking in college—a practice that continued into law school—my disease turned on ... forever! Scientists cannot predict exactly when this "light switch" of addiction might flip on for any individual; however, they *have* proven that if you never drink or use drugs at all, the switch will stay in the "off" position forever.

During law school, I moved back in with my parents. Although this made drinking more difficult, I managed to continue with it. In my last year of law school, I got married and moved in with my wife. Soon, I found myself sneaking drinks at night "to help me sleep." Helping myself get to sleep was how I justified my drinking to others and myself. The disease of addiction has sneaky ways of making you think you do not have it. It convinces you that what you're doing is justified. In college, my nightly drinking was "normal" because "everyone does it;" after I got married, my nightly drinking (which I hid from my wife and others) was "necessary" for me to get to sleep.

Work

Year after year, my disease worsened. What started as a few nightly beers turned into five to ten drinks of hard alcohol. I felt sick almost every morning and took naps at lunch instead of eating. It is a miracle I maintained a successful career during this time.

Fatherhood

The drinking only worsened after children came. Although kids are terrific, being a father is stressful. That provided my disease with another excuse to drink! By this time, if I didn't drink every night I'd go through withdrawals and not be able to get to sleep. Therefore, all my nights included drinking some form of alcohol— whether at Dave & Buster's or from the little alcohol bottles I packed for business trips.

It was during that ten-year span that I realized I was an alcoholic. I came up with excuse after excuse to drink, even while making daily promises never to drink again. The addiction took over, and no matter what I told myself in the morning, by late afternoon I was satisfied with some half-witted justification for why I needed to drink that night.

The Dry County

Although the realization that I was under the control of a disease developed over many years, one moment sticks out in my mind. It occurred on an innocent business trip to Texas, one of hundreds I made during my business career. I landed in the mid-afternoon twilight of Austin and took a taxi to the nearby town of Killeen. On the way, I asked the cab driver to stop by a liquor or convenience store for some "snacks." Of course, "snacks" meant beer, which had become a staple in my travels.

What I didn't know was that that particular county was "dry": stores there were not permitted to sell any form of alcohol on Sundays. I left the shop with water and candy, and I told myself this was not a big deal; after all, I'd gone many nights before without any alcohol. Unfortunately, my disease did not agree. I tossed and turned the entire night, unable to sleep for even one minute. That was when I realized that drinking alcohol had become something more than a bad habit.

Unfortunately, knowing you're an alcoholic and stopping the progression of the disease are two very different things. After that sleepless night, I would need seven more years of drinking before I sought help.

For years, the material and family successes around me had provided my disease with convenient excuses: "Hey, you're not that bad off. You have a great wife, two great kids, a great house, and a great job. It's not like you're living on the street, right?" This type of thinking allowed me to believe I was coping fairly well.

Even so, I started praying for relief from my addiction. This lasted for about five years. Thankfully, my prayers were finally answered, and I was able to ask for the help I needed.

So you can trust me when I tell you this yet again: *people with the disease of addiction cannot control it.*

We addicts are overwhelmed by our disease, which, unless we get help, always progresses in the stages detailed here. Willpower and "trying hard" cannot beat it. I've succeeded in everything else I have done in life—school, work, career—but I could not beat this disease once it caught hold. Not without professional help. But *you* can beat it ... by never letting it start.

Think about all the successful and wealthy people who have, over the years, died from drug abuse: Elvis Presley, Heath Ledger, Whitney Houston, Michael Jackson, Marilyn Monroe, and Cory Monteith (from *Glee*), to name a few. Although these people had access to the best doctors in the world, they all ended up dying. No matter how strong-willed you are, the disease is stronger yet. It's like cancer: without medical assistance, it will eventually kill you.

Thoughts from Lianna

During my dad's addictive stage, I felt strange at first because I didn't understand what was going on. When I was told that my dad had this disease, I finally saw how differently he was acting. I noticed that he was not finding as much joy in playing with my brother and me as he had before; he wanted to be alone all the time. I also remember him leaving the house much too often to cool down because he was angry or upset. Sometimes he would leave and not come home for hours. In fact, he wasn't home most of the time. I knew he didn't intend to be so quick-tempered, but as I've learned since then, this sort of behavior comes with drug and alcohol addiction.

Even if your parent's behavior is changing, that doesn't mean his or her feelings about you will change. Your parent will always love you; the disease is stopping him or her from showing his or her feelings effectively. This aspect of addiction is difficult even for me to understand: it's like the addiction becomes more important than anything else in the world. Every day, the addict drinks to keep the disease happy.

Addicts become blind to the things that really matter in life: family and friends.

My parents fought a lot. Almost every day, I heard yelling coming from upstairs. Sometimes I would worry; other times I would just tune out the voices. I was young when my dad was drinking, so I didn't understand as much as I do now.

Now I realize they were fighting because the disease was changing my dad. Addiction made him more aggressive, until it seemed as if he was always looking for a fight. No wonder my parents fought all the time. I don't know the scientific way to explain how addiction contributes to this aggression, but my parents definitely bumped heads.

Devotional Messages

"They close up their callous hearts, and their mouths speak with arrogance. They have tracked me down, they now surround me, with eyes alert, to throw me to the ground. They are like a lion hungry for prey, like a fierce lion crouching in cover." —Psalm 17:10–12

I mean for this devotional message to refer to your addicted parent/guardian. He or she is becoming arrogant and fierce at this stage.

"Lo, this is the man that made not God his strength; but trusted in the abundance of his riches, and strengthened himself in his wickedness."
—Psalm 52:7

CHAPTER
6

My Feelings

Whatever you're feeling now is the right way to feel. Angry, scared, hopeless, alone, resentful—it's all okay. You might even be skeptical of what Lianna and I are telling you. After all, you don't really know us. And what does our story have to do with you, with your life? You may be thinking, "I don't drink. I don't do drugs. What does this have to do with me?" But the reality is, the pressure on you to try drugs and alcohol will grow over the next few years, and the majority of kids give in to it at some point.

If you are dealing with a family member who is addicted, don't feel bad or guilty about your feelings. You didn't choose to have a family member become an addict. You

didn't choose to have this disease affect your family. And most of all, you did not choose to have addiction in your own genes.

Kids your age are not trained professionals and do not know how to deal with addiction, much less with an addicted family member. But you know what? Millions of children are going through exactly what you're going through today; you are not alone.

It's important that you feel a sense of power and confidence with the knowledge you are gaining from this book. You can prevent the disease from entering and ruining your life. Things are not hopeless even if your dad, grandfather, and great-grandfather have all been alcoholics. Things are not hopeless even if all of your sisters and brothers have problems with alcohol or other substances. With the knowledge you have now, you can break the cycle. And if you have no family history of substance abuse, you can keep it that way.

Now that you understand that addiction is a disease that people cannot simply turn off, you might want to view what others do with a sense of concern rather than anger. It's easy to be angry at an addict. Even I still feel that way about some addicts ... until I remind myself that inside each addict is a nice person being controlled by a powerful disease.

If you are living with an addict remember, addicts don't act the way they do because of anything *you* did, or because they hate you. The disease is in control; you're an innocent victim. I know it's hard to accept this outlook, so during times of trouble in your house, try to remember this simple fact: your mom or dad loves you. It is the disease of addiction that's treating you so poorly.

Hopefully, what you're learning from this book will help you transform your feelings of hopelessness, anger, hatred, and confusion into understanding, confidence, and hope.

Let Them Out

But remember, feelings are not something you can entirely control. Although we addicts try to manage our feelings with drugs and alcohol, feelings are nothing more than chemical reactions in the brain. When you cry while watching a sad movie, that's your brain working its magic. You have little choice in it.

In the same way, if your dad has been ignoring you more and more often, or treating you worse over the years, you're bound to feel hurt, angry, alone, and resentful. These feelings will not go away quickly.

I know for a fact that when an addict chooses drugs over his children, it is the disease making that choice, not the person. Most parents unconditionally love their children and would not deliberately make such choices. During my active addiction (when I was still drinking alcohol), I failed to put my children first. My disease made me put alcohol first and my children second.

So if you have a parent who is treating you this way, it's okay to be angry. It's okay to cry. It's okay to want a better parent. And it's okay to tell him or her your feelings; let those feelings out.

Try your best to rid yourself of guilt. You are no more at fault for what's happening than a kid with a mother who has breast cancer is responsible for her disease.

Remember, too, that if you choose to get involved in substance abuse, your attitude and actions towards those who love you will also change. You will be hurting yourself, but you will eventually also be hurting those you love. First will come the changes in your personality; the way you treat your family and friends will suffer, and you will not be able to avoid letting them down and hurting their feelings. Eventually, as the alcohol or drugs begin to diminish your health and destroy your body, you will hurt them on a whole new level. They will worry about you, feel guilt and frustration for not being able to help you, and then sadness for your plight. So, before you take that first drink or try that first drug ask yourself—who might I be hurting besides myself?

Thoughts from Lianna

How are you feeling? Really think about that. I did, and how I felt was very uncomfortable, as if I didn't even know my dad anymore. That's natural. This is a tough time for you and your parent. It's really important to know how you're feeling and to recognize and acknowledge these feelings. Here's a tip that helped me: always remember that your parent loves and cares for you, no matter what.

Devotional Message

"I cried out to God for help; I cried out to God to hear me. When I was in distress, I sought the Lord."
—Psalm 77:1–2a

You might feel distress, as well as fear, anger, or sadness. In tough times, I cry, and I pray to God for help because I know that He is there for me. I always want Him to hear my pleas. You, too, should seek help from God, especially when you need it the most.

7

Does He Have a Disease?

There is no doubt that using alcohol or drugs can lead to disease. Liver disease, heart disease, hepatitis, and a host of other diseases are associated with prolonged or careless substance abuse. But the most insidious disease of all, the one we most often deny falling prey to, is addiction.

Once again, it's time for good news/bad news. I'll start with the good: yes, people can stop drinking or using drugs. There's a solution (discussed later in this book) that millions of people have used. Make no mistake; it's very hard to do. It takes a lifetime of effort, but it's possible. If someone isn't using drugs today, then hopefully he's "cured" for today and will work hard every new day never to use drugs again. If he *is* still using drugs today, hopefully he will someday find the strength to ask for help and follow the steps needed for recovery.

> ... because addiction is a disease that affects your mind, it can convince you that you don't have a disease at all!

The problem—the bad news—is that because addiction is a disease that affects your mind, it can convince you that you don't have a disease at all! Even as it makes you seek out drugs daily, it persuades you that nothing is wrong. This double whammy is one of the many reasons addiction is so difficult to overcome.

> Realizing that you have a disease over which you have no control is a shock that can save your life.

Thus, someone in the middle of an addiction might not even realize she has a disease. She might think, "Everyone drinks, so, why shouldn't I?" Or "I have anxiety, so I need to drink." Or "I work hard, so why can't I drink at night?" Or "All my friends drink. Why shouldn't I?" But eventually most addicts realize it's not really a choice: they *have* to drink or use drugs. They have no control over their need.

CAUTION: CURVES AHEAD!

Realizing that you have a disease over which you have no control is a shock that can save your life. This happened to me on my first day of rehab, when I was told that addiction is a disease and shown scientific facts explaining why. What a relief that was! Instantly, decades of guilt vanished. I could blame the *disease*, not my willpower.

Today, as you read this, you do not have an active disease. But it may be hiding in your genes, and without prevention it will probably become active. No one can tell you exactly when. Will it be after you try just one drug, or after you "experiment" for five years? Will it happen after three months of heavy drinking, or after five years of moderate drinking? No one knows.

However, most addicts realize too late that they have a disease. I was in my thirties before I grasped that I couldn't stop drinking. By then, the disease was permanently activated. My sister's best friend recognized her addiction during her mid-thirties, but by then her liver was so diseased that she died. Many addicts never acknowledge their addictions, and they end up in jail, in mental institutions, or in a grave.

What I can say about all addicts is this: we could have benefitted from the knowledge in this book, had someone shared it with us before we ever started using any drugs or alcohol. Unfortunately, parents usually lack this knowledge, and families of addicts are often particularly reluctant to talk about anything as serious as disease. I'm convinced that this simple piece of knowledge may have saved thousands or millions of people from addiction. The good news is, now *you* have that knowledge.

Swinging at the Screwball

I recently read baseball player Josh Hamilton's autobiography about his struggles with drugs and alcohol. The most amazing thing about his story is how quickly his disease took over. Josh had never used alcohol or drugs before he was twenty. He was considered the best high school baseball player of all time and was a very happy and polite young man. Then a friend invited him out for his first beer. That same night, he tried drugs for the first time. Four years later, he was almost dead! Think about that: twenty years without any drugs or alcohol, and then a single, simple decision led to ruin.

What if Josh had known he had a disease that could steal from him everything he had gained—all because he drank a single beer? What if the thought of losing his baseball career was in his mind when his friend invited him out? Would he have accepted the invitation? Although I do not know Josh, my guess is he would have said no.

Thoughts from Lianna

If you realize your parent or guardian does have the disease of addiction, it might be hard to deal with at first. But you can find a way to push through, like my dad and I did.

This disease does not go away instantly, so you have to be patient. It can take a long time for your family member to recover. It took my dad a month to recuperate in rehab after about ten years of serious drinking.

The disease receded for my dad because he was so willing to change. He knew that recovery was the right decision, and he was willing to change for himself and our family.

Just like other diseases, addiction can take a while to dissipate. It requires medical help and a lot of patience from everyone.

Devotional Message

"My God, my God, why have you forsaken me?"
—Matthew 27:46b

You might feel anger toward God if your parent is an addict, but He only gives people choices. Your family member just made the wrong choice and slid into the darkness of drugs or alcohol. I try not to see addiction as a curse; I try to see it a blessing because it built my dad's spirit and gave me a chance to share this with you.

Am I Different from An Addict?

Yes, you *are* different! Different than you were when you began reading this book. You are now empowered by knowledge that your dad or mom did not have at your age. It's that simple. Unlike him or her, you know that whether you have a genetic predisposition towards addiction, if you avoid alcohol and drugs, the disease of addiction will never take over your life. You also know

that because the disease may be hidden in your genes without any sign of addiction in your family, avoiding drugs and alcohol is also the smart and safe approach. Of course, this may be a difficult task, but at least you have information that most children don't have.

Environment and genetics do play a role in whether or not we succumb to addiction. In fact, they play a role in many of the decisions we make in our lives. And understanding this empowers us to avoid their influence when it is negative.

Kids are products of their parents, good and bad. Think about all the things you like to do that your dad or mom also likes to do. Do you like the same foods, the same movies, the same books? Do you play the same sports? Do you have the same type of temper? Are you both left-handed?

> Environment and genetics do play a role in whether or not we succumb to addiction. In fact, they play a role in many of the decisions we make in our lives.

What I have learned in years of therapy and sobriety (being sober means not using drugs or, for me, drinking alcohol) is that we are all very similar to our parents. If our parents are emotional, so are we. If our parents react in anger, so do we. If our parents went to college and are smart, so are we. If our parents run from feelings and never discuss them, so do we. And, unfortunately, if our parents have the disease of addiction, so do we.

I certainly fit this picture. My parents never dealt with emotional issues, and neither did I. My parents both went to college, and so did I. My dad drinks, and so did I. My mom's family is full of addicts, and I am an addict.

I also see that my children are much like me. Lianna is great in school, as was I. Lianna loves fruits and vegetables, as do I. Bennett loves football and rap music, as do I. But there's an important difference. Through this book and other work, both kids can say, "Dad is an alcoholic—but I am not."

More than eight years ago, I started my journey of recovery and quest for knowledge. Today, I'm different from most of my relatives. I also understand why I'm different from my friends who can drink normally. I understand why for years I chose alcohol over my kids and wife, and made the other selfish, irrational decisions I made. I understand that I am an addict.

But most importantly, my kids are not like me because they understand addiction. They know they cannot drink like a normal person. They understand that by simply staying away from drugs and alcohol, they can avoid the pain that has affected tens of millions of people in this world. They understand that a week or a year—or even one moment—of using drugs could permanently activate their slumbering disease. They also understand that with their help, the disease might one day be trimmed from our family tree.

My wonderful children now have the knowledge to make a choice of sobriety—knowledge that most addicts never receive until it is too late.

Thoughts from Lianna

You are different from everyone else—at your school, on your sports teams—so why would you not also be different in terms of potential for addiction?

You're different from addicts because you can learn not to give in to alcohol and drugs before the addiction even has the chance to start. You're different because you can help the disease—that is, you can help it stay away.

You're also different from addicts in other ways. You know now that they have a disease. Though your addicted parent, friend, or loved one might say things that hurt you, you know that that's just the addiction taking over. You know you aren't to blame. And you know that you don't have to go down the same path of addiction that your parent took.

You are completely different from your parent because you have knowledge about addiction. You have been told what it can do to you and your life, and you know that you can make the right decision when it comes to drugs and alcohol.

Devotional Message

"Also, it is not good for a person to be without knowledge, and he who makes haste with his feet errs." —Proverbs 19:2

God meant for humans to learn from their mistakes and to make good choices. But we aren't perfect. I know it's hard to always make the right decisions, but this is a choice you must make. You can stay away from drugs, or you can choose addiction. You can always look to God for guidance when it comes time to make a choice.

9

Why Can't He Stop?

Most addicts cannot stop drinking or using drugs on their own. That may sound strange, but it's true. Look at what people give up in their lives for their disease, and ask yourself if anyone would actually *choose* those results:

- Actor Heath Ledger played the Joker in *Batman: The Dark Knight*, as well as other highly acclaimed roles. He died from abusing prescription pills. Would he have *deliberately* chosen death in order to have his pills?

- Actress Lindsay Lohan has spent years of her life in rehab, prison, and controversy. Would she deliberately *choose* those things over the life of a movie star?

- Super-Star Prince had all the money, talent and fame in the world and lost his life to addiction alone in an elevator. Whitney Houston was found dead, alone in her own bathtub. Certainly, they would have chosen a different path.

- Josh Hamilton was named an All-Star player in Major League Baseball five times. But his path to fame took a five-year detour into drugs, and he ended up living in a trailer using drugs all day instead of playing baseball. Would he have actually *chosen* to live in a trailer with criminals instead of pursuing his million-dollar baseball career?

> One of the basic principles of addiction recovery is that the addict must admit he or she is not in control of his or her addiction; he or she is powerless over it.

Can you imagine choosing a drink over your mom? Over your sister? But this is what happens to millions of people. *The disease makes the choice for them.*

One of the basic principles of addiction recovery is that the addict must admit he or she is not in control of his or her addiction; he or she is powerless over it. That's why addicts need professional help to quit. Yet even addicts who go into rehabilitation centers have less than a 30 percent chance of staying sober for a year. It's that hard. Think about it: out of every one hundred addicts who spend thirty, sixty, or ninety days in a full-time rehabilitation center, seventy or more will relapse within the first year.

As for the addicts who do *not* go into rehabilitation, their chances of recovery are even smaller.

So, when you think about alcohol or drugs as just a rite of passage, just something all kids try, think about this, too. And if you have a family member or loved one who is an addict, when your frustration with them grows, remember this: they are not picking the disease over you. They really aren't.

In Denial

Do you remember another reason addicts can't stop? It's because the disease convinces them they don't have a disease in the first place. This is commonly known as "denial." The addict denies—to others and to him - or herself—that he or she has a problem with drugs or alcohol.

This happens with every addict. An alcoholic hiding vodka bottles around the house rationalizes the behavior as *protecting his wife*. A drug addict stealing

to get money for heroin justifies the act as *necessary for his well-being*. The addict's brain has a good excuse for any behavior.

It's quite likely that the addict honestly believes he is not an addict, even though everyone around him knows better. Only through treatment and sobriety can an addicted person see the truth.

Unfortunately, sometimes an addict's family *also* denies reality. The addict in denial spreads the denial among his or her family members. Lies become normal, and parents, wives, friends, and others begin believing the lies so they can live with the behavior.

Examples of this process are common in every family. A heroin user tells his mom he has the flu. A wife who comes home stumbling drunk tells her husband she has food poisoning. The lie is accepted by the person hearing it, and in this way denial spreads throughout the family, making recovery that much more difficult for everyone.

Every single morning for ten years, I would ask myself why I'd drunk so much the night before. It was as if when I drank, a different person took over my mind and wouldn't let me stop drinking. Was it the devil? An alter ego?

Why couldn't I just *not have had that drink*? Surely it was an easy choice. After all, I could do almost anything else I set my mind to. If I wanted to get an A in a class, I could do it. If I needed to drive ten hours as a favor for a friend, I could do it. If I needed to make more money to buy a new car, I could do it. Yet I couldn't stop drinking!

On many mornings, feeling terribly sick from the night before, I would come up with detailed plans to help me stop drinking. Some of these schemes were so silly I now laugh at them:

- Drink only on weekends.

- Drink only beer.

- Drink only after 7:00 at night.

- Drink only at home.

- Never drink more than five beers.

All of these plans failed miserably. I wasn't the only one to ever try this sort of thing; most addicts think they can produce the world's first cure for addiction. Most addicts go through pitiful attempts to stop the disease. It never works. The simple fact is that an addict can never drink like a normal person—*ever*.

I bet you know people who have other bad habits that are hard to stop, such as nail biting or cracking their knuckles. Difficult urges to conquer ... but nothing like trying to beat addiction.

Thoughts from Lianna

At first, I didn't realize my dad had the disease of addiction. Maybe you didn't realize your parent has a disease, either. But once I did realize it, I wanted to say something to him about it because I thought he would simply stop if I asked him to.

Sadly, it doesn't work that way. Addicts reach a point where they aren't able to stop, even at the cost of hurting their loved ones, because the disease has taken over completely. That's a hard concept to wrap your head around, but I think that by this point in the book, you realize that it's true: they *can't* stop.

Addiction is in their genes ... your genes ... my genes. I like to think of eye color to understand this. My mom has brown eyes; my dad has brown eyes. I got my brown eyes from my parents. I didn't ask for brown eyes; I just got them. You can't control your genes, so if that disease that is in your genes gets a hold of you, you can't stop it. I know that this might be scary to think about, but you'll be okay. Everyone in your life is there to help you, and you can prevent this gene from coming alive.

Once addicts start drinking or using drugs, it's hard for them to break the cycle because of "denial"; they don't even realize they have a problem. My dad needed to go to rehab before he could acknowledge that he had the disease of addiction. That acknowledgement, along with the efforts of the doctors in rehab, helped him begin the recovery process. I couldn't help him, but I could be strong at home and make sure I never turned on the disease in my own genes. Your parents love you. Keep your faith in them and don't ever switch on the disease in your genes.

Devotional Message

". . . for my door was always open to the traveler."
—Job 31:32b

God says this, but your family member(s) may not choose to enter the door of redemption. It might be too hard for them. If so, just try to counsel them in their important decisions, and show them that you will always be by their side to offer love and support.

10

To Whom Do I Talk If I Have an Addicted Parent?

This book isn't meant to provide a miracle cure to prevent addiction. As you know by now, there *is* no miracle cure. What this book does is give you the knowledge necessary to *avoid* addiction. But life is unpredictable. You might hit bumps in the road. You might run into situations where drugs and alcohol are an easy choice, a temptation. You might face peer pressure. Your friends might be drinking beer and want you to join in. You might be at a party where everyone is doing drugs. Or you might have a personal difficulty that leaves you feeling depressed and looking for relief.

If you encounter moments in life where you're tempted to start using drugs or alcohol, you need to talk to someone. Or if you're having a hard time dealing with addiction in your family and need help, you need to talk to someone about it.

Remember, if your parent's or other loved one's behavior is an issue, you can't fix it—but talking about it might make you feel guilty or ashamed. Such feelings are normal for someone living with an addict, but they aren't fair. It might be helpful to talk with someone about such emotions.

> Most of us turn to our friends for help when we find ourselves in difficult situations.

If you are experiencing peer pressure to try drugs or alcohol, and you are experiencing anxiety about it and finding it difficult to handle, it might also be helpful to speak with someone about what you are experiencing.

Most of us turn to our friends for help when we find ourselves in difficult situations. But you are still young, and so are your friends. While their experience in dealing with these situations might be similar to yours, their experience in handling and resolving them is also as limited as yours. Thus, while your friends might give you comfort, you cannot count on them for the best advice.

To whom should you talk? There is no perfect answer. There is also no wrong answer. However, keeping your feelings to yourself in this difficult time is definitely not the *best* answer.

Here are some ideas about people you could talk to:

- **Your addicted parent:** This might seem strange and difficult to do, but as we've said before, even addicted parents love their children unconditionally. It is often this very love that makes the addict seek treatment for his or her addiction, so if you're becoming angry and scared because of someone's addiction, tell him or her.

- **Your non-addicted parent:** If you have an addict parent who is still married to a "normal" parent, this is a natural place to start. Your "normal" parent might be feeling many of the same things you are. He possibly feels unloved, angry, and betrayed. She might feel her spouse's problem is her fault. So, talk to that parent and share your feelings with him or her. It could be a moment in which you two bond and share, which will help both of you. But keep in mind that your non-addicted parent might also be in denial. As you have learned, denial is a common trait in almost all addictions—for both the addict and non-addicted family members. If your non-addicted parent doesn't want to listen to your feelings, or doesn't agree with you, that's okay. There are other people you can talk to.

- **School counselors:** The counselors at your school are there to help you through rough times, and dealing with an addicted parent is a very rough time. Don't be ashamed to make an appointment and talk to a counselor; that is his or her job, one he or she chose to do. He or she wants to help you.

- **Priest, rabbi, or other religious leader:** Do you attend church or synagogue? If so, a priest or other religious leader is a great choice for sharing your feelings.

- **Other relatives:** Sharing feelings with a trusted relative is better than keeping them bottled up. If you have a grandparent or an aunt or uncle you are close to, spend some time with him or her discussing your feelings about your addicted parent.

- **Other adults:** If you are close with other adults, such as a teacher or a friend's parent, this may be a good choice for you.

- **Groups such as Al-Anon:** Al-Anon supports family members of addicts and has a website with lots of advice and ways for you to get help: www.al-anon. alateen.org

In my own life, my children's influence and remarks of concern about my addiction are what ultimately drove me to seek help. That's how I know it's important for you to tell your parent that you're concerned about his or her drinking or drug use. Still, don't expect your parent to suddenly change his or her behavior. Most likely, denial will kick in, and he or she will try to convince you that he or she doesn't have a problem with drinking or drugs.

On the other hand, it's also possible your distress will change his or her life. My daughter's concern changed mine.

"Daddy Drank a Lot"

It seems so crazy now. Looking back on the course of my disease, I had five hundred experiences—no, a thousand—a million!—that should have made me ask for help. Whether it was falling and smashing my head on a bathtub, throwing up all day long, screaming at my wife, or driving drunk, any of these horrible consequences should have made me seek help. But I was in denial. That's how strong and sneaky the disease is; it takes over your mind and convinces you that you are normal. So, for twenty years I lived with the disease, barely surviving, not seeking help. Until one concerned statement from my daughter finally got through to me, and I went into rehab.

"Daddy drank a lot" was the simple comment Lianna made to my wife to describe a concert I had attended with her. We'd gone to see her favorite *American Idol* singer, David Archuleta. I'd surprised her with great tickets months earlier and had so looked forward to this daddy/daughter day. You see, even during the worst of my drinking days I valued my role as a father. In fact, I was able to look past my diminishing health, marriage, and happiness because of these occasional moments of fun, gifts, and joy with my children.

This particular weekend, I planned for the two of us to attend the event we had talked about nonstop for weeks. Although during the prior few years I had developed a pattern of taking limousines to concerts (knowing full well that I would get drunk), I was so dedicated to making this a great daddy/daughter event that I decided to drive. And yet, after what I believed to be an amazing daddy/daughter day, I was crushed by Lianna's assessment of the experience: "Daddy drank a lot."

These moments of "fun" and gifts were the Band-Aid masking the fact that my life was on a path of destruction. Lianna's comment violently ripped the Band-Aid off. I was left bleeding and desperate—and less than a week later, I checked myself into rehab.

Your care and concern might be what is needed to inspire the addict to bring forward the loving parent that's inside him or her, but that he or she has pushed into the background for too long. Even if it's only for a moment, that might be long enough to allow your dad or mom – or friend or loved one – to ask for help.

No one can say if hearing from you will be the thing that helps your parent get sober. And his or her sobriety is not your responsibility anyway. But simply saying, "Dad, I worry about your drinking," might be enough to help your dad realize what his disease is doing to you.

Thoughts from Lianna

When my dad was drinking, I talked to my mom. I told her everything I thought she needed to know.

One night, my dad took me to a concert where they were giving out small glasses of beer. I remember Dad going back and forth to the stand, over and over again. When we got home, my mom asked me how many drinks he had had that night. I trusted her to listen to me and comfort me, so I told her the truth: "Six or seven." Later, she told me that when she had asked Dad the same question, he replied, "Two."

Although I didn't know it at the time, this was the event that pushed my father to check himself into rehab.

Find someone you love and trust and can talk to. That one person may not have all the answers you need, but he or she will be able to help and console you. You shouldn't have to hold all of your feelings in. Not only is it *important* to talk to someone in tough times, but you have a *right* to talk to someone and to get advice.

Devotional Message

"They will pass through the sea of trouble."
—Zechariah 10:11a

Your addicted parent will pass through the "sea of trouble,"
and you will, too. But you can always talk to God. He is there
for you.

Peer Pressure

For most kids, the first offer of drugs or alcohol comes from their peers—friends or schoolmates. If your friends or other kids at school are doing something and try to make you do it too, you are experiencing peer pressure. Imagine that a bully convinces you to make fun of a weaker kid, or your friends are wearing a certain brand of shoes and you want to wear them too, or someone is making fun of a singer or movie star and so you go along, even if you secretly like that singer or movie star. All of these are forms of giving in to peer pressure.

Peer pressure is a very powerful force, for people of all ages, and it's difficult to overcome. But there is a way. And knowing that using alcohol or drugs can lead to addiction, or that you have a disease in your genes that definitely could predispose you to addiction, should make dealing with peer pressure much easier to manage.

Remember, while some kids have addiction in their families and therefore could have a genetic predisposition towards becoming addicted, just because you don't seem to have a family history of addiction does not mean you are definitely in the clear. The disease may very well be hiding in your DNA and you may have the allergy as much as my children do.

Peer pressure is a very powerful force, for people of all ages, and it's difficult to overcome.

Peanuts, Sugar, Smoke

Think about a person with a peanut allergy. Is it hard for him to pass up a brownie that contains peanuts when he knows that eating it could kill him? No. Or think about a classmate with diabetes: do kids pressure him to eat chocolate? Probably not. How about the kid who has asthma? Do kids pressure him to smoke? Not likely. Knowing what alcohol and drugs can lead to should be enough to keep you substance-free. Knowing that you have a disease—or the potential for a disease—gives you a built-in excuse to go against peer pressure. Use this excuse if you have a family member that is an addict or

not. You very well may have had a great grandfather that was an alcoholic and your allergy to alcohol is as real as mine.

Keep that in mind. When someone offers you a beer or drug, simply answer, "No, thanks, I'm allergic." "No thanks, I have a family history of addition I'm going to pass." "Sorry dude, alcoholism runs in my family I will have to pass."

... if people keep pushing you, they're not really your friends, are they?

When I was in high school, I used my childhood asthma as an excuse not to smoke cigarettes. When someone pressured me to smoke with him or her, I'd say, "No, thanks, I have asthma. I can't." Imagine if, a few years later, I had known that I had the disease of addiction in my genes! I could have said, "No, thanks," to alcohol, too.

When someone offers you alcohol or drugs, simply answer, "No, I'm allergic to that," and move on.

Will saying "No, thanks" always be enough to stop a peer from pressuring you? Sadly, no. But if people keep pushing you, they're not really your friends, are they? Would a true friend make you eat peanuts if you had a peanut allergy? No. A true friend wouldn't pressure you to take something you're allergic to, either.

Think about how this excuse could have worked for Josh Hamilton, the baseball player we talked about earlier in this book. He was a superstar high school baseball player who had never tried drugs or alcohol. He was on a path to superstardom when, at the age of nineteen, he was offered a beer by a friend he was hanging out with. Drinking that first simple beer activated his addiction. In only a few months, after nineteen years of living without drugs and alcohol, this promising baseball star lost his career to drugs and alcohol and became a homeless addict.

What if Josh had been armed with the knowledge that you now have? "Sorry, dude," he might have said, "I'm allergic to beer. Want to go to the batting cages tonight?" Maybe then Josh Hamilton would be known today as "the best baseball player in the world," instead of "the best baseball player who is an addict."

Think of it this way: you know that if there is addiction in your family, you have an allergy to alcohol and drugs, and that if you don't have addiction in your family, you still might be susceptible and it might be hidden in your family anyway. And people who are allergic to something should never be pressured into using it. Do not be ashamed; be proud and strong.

I wish I could say that this is the *perfect* solution for peer pressure, but life doesn't work like that. You might still be coerced to do other things you don't have a built-in reason to refuse, such as stealing candy from a store or toilet papering someone's house. It's hard to claim that you're allergic to shoplifting or pranking. But now you have the perfect excuse to avoid the type of peer pressure this book is about: the kind that pushes you to use drugs or alcohol.

"I can't, man, I'm allergic to it."

It's that simple.

Thoughts from Lianna

There are many forms of peer pressure. You feel it at school, in sports, or when people encourage you to use drugs. The way my aunt got started with drugs was when her friends in high school urged her to try them.

If you see other people doing bad things, don't follow them. Simply say no and walk away. By now, you know better than to take drugs. Even if the popular kids are doing so, or you want to do whatever your friends are doing, please, just don't.

In class, I learned the "No, Go, Tell" rule. According to this rule, first you say no, then you leave, then you tell an adult. In the future, you should make an effort to practice something like this to help you stay away from drugs.

Devotional Message

"As for the deeds of men—by the word of your lips
I have kept myself from the ways of the violent."
—Psalm 17:4

Stay away from the things you know are wrong, especially if you see your friends or family giving in to the "ways of the violent."

You may be around people who are making bad decisions. That doesn't mean they're bad people, but you shouldn't give in to any form of peer pressure that pushes you to drink or do drugs, ever.

CHAPTER
12

How Will I Fit In?

Millions of people in the world don't drink or use drugs. In fact, some religions forbid all forms of alcohol and drug use, yet most of the people in those religions manage to live happy, healthy lives. The Mormon and Islamic religions are two of the most notable examples. Mormons and Muslims are not supposed to have a single drink of alcohol or take one illicit drug during their lives. Worldwide, more than a billion people practice these religions. Yes, *a billion*, as in 1,000,000,000. If a billion people can avoid alcohol and drugs for their entire lives, and you know that you should do the same thing to avoid a life-threatening disease, isn't it possible that you, too, can stay free of alcohol and drugs?

Sometimes your friends don't need to pressure you by bugging you or trying to push alcohol into your hands. Sometimes you pressure *yourself* because you want to fit in.

I know that feeling. I was afraid that if I got sober, I wouldn't fit in with my friends, family, and coworkers who did drink. Would it feel weird? Would I have to change my job? Would I have to get new friends? How would I attend family events where alcohol was available? What would I do when people toasted the bride and groom at a wedding?

It turns out I didn't need to be afraid. My family and my true friends love *me*, not the beer that was always in my hand.

Sometimes at parties or functions, someone will ask me, "Why aren't you drinking?" Just as I advised you to tell people that you have an allergy to alcohol, I come right out and tell them the truth: "Addiction runs in my family and is a battle I cannot win." Every person I've said that to—every single one—has respected me for saying it. In fact, they often congratulate me or say, "Wow, I wish I could be that strong." Once people know you have a disease that you are trying to avoid, peer pressure should go away and a sense of pride should replace it. You're using your knowledge to help yourself. If you run into someone who makes fun of you because of this, you are better off without that "friend."

A lot of addicts worry about how they'll fit in with other people if they get sober, because "All my friends do it." I understand. My social world revolved around beer and wine. My business travels and dinner meetings always involved alcohol. Almost all of my friends drink beer or wine at social events; so do almost all my relatives. I worried that I could never again hang around my friends, customers, coworkers, or relatives!

For you, saying no to drugs and alcohol might at first seem to separate you from your friends. But real friends have a lot more in common than substance use and abuse.

What actually happened is far from that. I continue to see most of the same people as before; I just don't drink with them. Some addicts cannot ever be around others who are drinking; it's just too uncomfortable. In that case, the addict might have to find new friends. Personally, I solved this problem by changing how I spend time with people: I don't go to bars with friends, which used to be a common pastime in my social and business circles. Instead, nowadays I might see a movie with coworkers on a business trip instead of chatting about the day's events over a beer. Or at a barbecue, I'll eat three servings of ribs instead of drinking all the beer I used to guzzle! I sure feel better the next day.

> Fitting in doesn't mean changing who you are; it means that people like you for *you.*

For you, saying no to drugs and alcohol might at first seem to separate you from your friends. But real friends have a lot more in common than substance use and abuse. They talk and play and share ideas. They study together, take hikes, surf, swim, play basketball, go to movies. There is a world of activities out there for you that have absolutely nothing to do with alcohol or drugs. Make friends with people who realize and take advantage of all the world has to offer. And keep those friends for life instead of the wrong crowd that loses friends to addiction along the way.

There is a world out there for you when you're free from drugs and alcohol. It might seem hard, but every addict will tell you that living without drugs and alcohol is easy; it's living as an addict that's hard.

Thoughts from Lianna

You, the kid reading this book, should never have a problem fitting in. You should always be yourself and never change the way you are just to fit in with anyone, especially right now.

You don't need to fit in with your addicted parents, because what they're doing is wrong. If you feel left out, excluded, or different, just talk about it with a family member. Don't feel like you're being forced into activating your disease. You know you're not. But also, don't feel pressured to share your life with people who are doing something you don't want to—and shouldn't—do. Make your own decisions.

Even in the future, when you're in high school or college, you don't have to feel peer pressured to do drugs along with your friends. Fitting in doesn't mean changing who you are; it means that people like you for *you*. It's so important to have friends who love who you are and don't want to change your personality.

Devotional Message

"You have heard a message from the Lord:
a letter was sent to the nations to say,
Rise, and let us go against him in battle."
—Obadiah 1:1b

In this case, you have to go against your family member. You don't need to fit in with your family member—or with your friend—if what he or she is doing is wrong—not now or ever.

CHAPTER
13

Is There a Cure?

Yes!!! The cure is simple: never let the disease start in the first place. Prevention is the only foolproof, 100 percent guaranteed, for-certain cure for addiction. That's good news! How many other diseases can be cured as simply? You can lower your chances of getting lung cancer by not smoking, but there's no way to prevent it entirely. Avoiding heart disease can be helped by good diet choices, but there is no way to completely prevent it, either. Science has developed shots that can prevent diseases such as polio, but even those take three or four inoculations from a doctor.

On the other hand, the disease of addiction can be prevented without any painful shots or gross medicine at all.

Unfortunately, avoiding the temptation of drugs and alcohol is not quite as easy as reading this book and putting it on your shelf. Life is complicated and unpredictable. But with your newfound knowledge, you have a much better chance of living your life disease-free than anyone who is addicted probably ever had.

You can prevent the disease from coming to life by using the very simple cure described in the previous chapter. But what happens to those addicts who are too late for that, who have already let the disease come alive? Is there a cure for them?

> Remember: the disease never dies; it just hides out, dormant, waiting to take control again.

Sadly, most doctors, addicts, and experts agree that there is no such thing as a cure for addiction. There is no pill to take, surgery to have, or test to pass that permanently heals an addict.

Don't despair, though. Even if it's too late for an addict to avoid taking that first drink, there are steps that are easy to follow that can make it possible for an addict to keep the disease away for the rest of his or her life. These steps include rehab, therapy, participating in groups such as Alcoholics Anonymous, and finding or rebuilding one's religious faith. Whichever path they choose, addicts must make an effort for the rest of their lives to keep the disease from taking over again. Remember: the disease never dies; it just hides out, dormant, waiting to take control again.

Look Both Ways

Hopefully this book has made you realize that you can take some simple actions *now* to avoid a lifelong fight with a powerful disease. Thinking about it that way, isn't it an easy choice?

All parents tell their kids to look both ways before crossing the street. I'm sure your parents told you never to go anywhere with strangers or even talk to strangers. And you may have already had a chat with your folks about the birds and the bees. Certainly, you have been trained over and over how to get to safety during a fire at school, and how to deal with an earthquake or hurricane. While these are serious events, for kids your age the potential—yet most avoidable—catastrophe you're most likely to face is addiction.

Despite this, I don't know a single addict who ever got a talk from his or her parents about the dangers of drug or alcohol use. Addiction is a terribly common (and increasing) problem in our schools and society; it should be getting much more attention than it does.

Thanks to the blessing of sobriety that I've had in the last few years, my children now have that knowledge— and now so do you.

The question "Is there a cure once you have an addiction?" is a great one. While the answer is no, a set of recovery steps is laid out for every addict who attends meetings at Alcoholics Anonymous, Narcotics Anonymous, or any similar group. These steps can change the addict's life (as they have mine), but they require daily effort. Yes, daily. In fact, these steps are so critical to the lives of millions of recovering addicts that we will examine them briefly later in this book. Knowledge is power, and you deserve to have power.

Thoughts from Lianna

Once the disease is active and takes over, the only "cure" for an addict is to get help. There is no medicine to cure addiction; all you can do is try to help the addict. Of course, it can be hard to help because you're scared or nervous that your parent might get mad. Your best way of helping is to speak out and state your opinion—maybe not directly to your parent, but to someone you trust. Teach your parent(s) and guide them. If you do that, it will bring them comfort and the feeling that someone can help them.

The only cure is in their hearts. If they realize they need to stop, they might do it—just as my dad did. The desire to stop the disease of addiction is very strong in some people; others need to be shown why to seek help.

My dad went to rehab for thirty days, a whole month. I remember visiting him. He always told me about fun activities he had done, such as yoga or crafts; every day we visited him he would give me something he'd made. I thank that rehab facility for helping my whole family. I'm so glad that my dad got the help he needed in time.

He just celebrated his eigth anniversary of being sober!

Devotional Message

"Do not let any unwholesome talk come out of your mouths, but only what is helpful for building others up according to their needs, that it may benefit those who listen." —Ephesians 4:29

God helps those who are truly faithful to Him. I prayed and prayed for my dad to get better. Beating addiction is tough, but it is definitely possible. Please try to help your family member. The only way to do so is to speak up. I told my mom about my dad's drinking, and look where we are now!

CHAPTER
14

God Is Calling Me to Help

For those of you who are religious, this chapter will be easy to read. For those of you who are not religious, it might not be so easy. Religion is one of those topics that is difficult to discuss or write about because people have different levels of belief, and different religions teach different things. Arguments based on religion are common. If you are feeling hopeless, you might even question the existence of God, and that is natural.

This chapter is not about whether or not there is a God. This chapter simply notes how a belief in God has played an important role in beating addiction for tens of millions of people. If you and your family are religious, this might help. If you are not, this won't hurt, and I hope you'll keep reading.

Experts generally agree that before the formation of Alcoholics Anonymous (or AA) almost a hundred years ago, an active addict faced very great odds in getting sober. The treatments recommended back then were all over the board. Magic potions, hypnosis, and other treatments surfaced all over the world to appeal to addicts desperate to stop. Addicts would travel for weeks, months, or years in search of a magical cure.

Of course, none of these magic pills worked, and doctors most often told an addict's family that the addict would end up dead, in jail, or in a mental institution.

With the creation of AA in Ohio in 1935, there was suddenly an approach that worked—for even the worst of alcoholics. This program quickly spread beyond Ohio to the entire United States and then the rest of the world; AA meetings can now be found all around the globe. Other groups such as Narcotics Anonymous (NA) were later formed for drug addicts.

What is the secret of these groups? They all follow two principles: (1) As part of a group, people can accomplish things an individual cannot. Someone sitting in a group of twenty other drug addicts has a much better chance of getting sober than he does sitting in his home, alone. And (2) the addict cannot cure himself or herself; he or she must ask God for help.

Thousands of books have been written about treatment and rehabilitation. The book you are reading today is intended to keep you away from addiction and the need for those other books. Just remember that a major component in these successful treatment programs is asking God for help. If you are hurting and want to try something that has worked for millions of others who have suffered the same way, try asking God for help.

I've heard it a thousand times in my own head and from other addicts who were still using drugs or alcohol: "Those people in AA groups are a bunch of religious nut jobs. God can't help me; only I can." And yet those who follow the steps of AA (which involve a belief in God and asking Him for help) seem to get better. Those who dismiss AA and NA groups, or God in general, do not seem to get better. (AA in fact doesn't even focus on God; it simply wants its members to realize that there is a "higher power" that guides our lives.) Those facts are good enough for me; I'm going with the winning approach.

Thoughts from Lianna

How can you help your addicted parent and yourself? That's a great question. I'm going to tell you a story, and you should think about this question as you read it.

In fourth grade, there was a lot of "girl drama" in my class. The new girl was being bullied. Day after day, I saw the other girls talking about her behind her back and even saying mean things to her face. I knew that this was not right; I had to do or say something. So, one day, I stood up to the bullies.

After that, the new girl was happier in our school environment; we became great friends. By the time I was in eighth grade, there was no more bullying in my class.

You shouldn't be afraid to do something about your situation. Of course, you have to respect your parents, but if you see something going on that you know isn't right, tell someone. By helping someone else, you are helping yourself.

Your future as part of a strong family should never be in jeopardy. For the sake of yourself and your family, don't be afraid to speak up.

Devotional Message

"I know that you can do all things,
your plans cannot be stopped."
—Job 42:2

The Lord has great plans for everyone, but you must choose which path to take. Right now, you have two paths to choose from: to help the addict by voicing your concern, or to just sit and watch. This is your choice.

15

Prescription Pills and The Opiate Epidemic

As we discussed earlier in this book, there are many prescription drugs which can be addictive. Addicts, in particular, should stay away from certain prescription pills, but so should anyone for whom they have not been prescribed. These pills have found their way into recreational use, with purveyors often telling us, "This is safe. It is from a doctor's prescription." Your friends might show up at a party with pills they took from their parents' medicine cabinet. Too many of these drugs at once can kill. Too many too often can lead to addiction. Only a doctor should dispense prescription drugs to you. And taking prescription drugs that are not yours to begin with is no different than drinking or taking any other drugs.

Our society views drugs obtained from doctors as acceptable, and drugs supplied by street dealers as illegal and dangerous. But for an addict there is little difference; an OxyContin pill from a doctor is the same as a dose of heroin from a street junkie. The addict's brain processes the two in the same manner, and drug addicts often transition to and from heroin and these pills. In fact, these days most heroin addicts start out by becoming addicted to pills and change to heroin because it can actually be cheaper.

Only a doctor should dispense prescription drugs to you. And taking prescription drugs that are not yours to begin with is no different than drinking or taking any other drugs.

A recent study by the Mayo Clinic showed that approximately 13 percent of Americans are on some sort of prescription antidepressants, and 13 percent are on prescription painkillers. This means that addictive prescriptions are in at least 26 percent of our medicine cabinets.

Pills that are addictive and so particularly dangerous include opiates (Vicodin, OxyContin, codeine) and "benzos" (Valium, Xanax). These pills have been proven to be extremely addictive, and they are very dangerous for anyone to use, and they are particularly dangerous for addicts to *ever* use. The brain reacts to them in a very similar manner as it does to illegal drugs and alcohol.

Opiates are painkillers. The name comes from "opium," which is processed out of the same plant that drug dealers use to produce heroin and other dangerous narcotics. Although opiates can be very helpful in controlling pain, they are so similar to heroin that they must be treated with extreme care. Millions of Americans are addicted to them. Recently our society has finally acknowledged that there now is an "opioid epidemic" across all parts of the United States and the world. In fact, on October 26, 2017, President Trump declared opioid abuse to be a public health emergency.

The damage that the opioid epidemic has caused is so large that it is difficult to comprehend. However, the statistics are so overwhelming that it should be easy for you to understand the danger. Here are just a few statistics on the crisis as of November 2017:

- Three million new Americans are becoming addicted to opiates each year.
- Between 1999 and 2015 the number of opioid deaths quadrupled.

- Every single day, 91 Americans die from an opioid overdose.

- More people die from opiates than in car crashes, from AIDS, or from guns.

- Opiate dependency can begin within A FEW DAYS OF INITIAL USE,

- 30% of teenagers that took opiates prescribed by a doctor (for a month) became addicted.

> It is very disheartening that we have known the danger inherent in these drugs for years, and yet they are still considered the primary treatment option for pain in the United States.

Obviously, opiate addiction is ravaging our country. The statistics above are only a brief glimpse into the problem. And remember if you have the addiction gene in your DNA (which you may be unaware of) the likelihood of becoming addicted to opiates only increases.

Until our society focuses on developing non-addictive pain killers these trends are almost certain to continue. It is very disheartening that we have known the danger inherent in these drugs for years, and yet they are still considered the primary treatment option for pain in the United States. Does this make sense to you? Can a country that uses drones for war, uses watches for emails, and travels in self-driving cars really not develop a pain pill that doesn't ruin the lives of 3 million people per year? The answer to that would require an entire book and would have to dive into the complex world of pharmaceutical companies, lobbyists and our government. For now, let's just concentrate on keeping opiates out of your body.

As with every other substance we talk about in this book, the good news is that you never have to start using opiates. Even a few days on the pills can lead to addiction. So, what should you do to avoid these pills? For one, if a doctor is going to prescribe opiates ask if something else, like Tylenol, would be sufficient. I asked this exact question a few years ago for a minor surgery and Tylenol worked fine. I did this to avoid becoming addicted, and because when I have taken opiates in the past, I was one of many people that hated how they made me feel.

If you are a parent reading this you have some to-do's as well. First, if you have opiates in your home, lock them in a safe. As we have discussed, opiates kill more people than guns. If you don't lock your opiates securely, you might as well be leaving a loaded gun for your kids to play with on top of their X-Box. You also need to be your child's advocate and protector from doctors looking to prescribe opiates. Tylenol or Advil are sufficient for most injuries and minor surgeries, and it is your responsibility, not the doctor's, to make sure your children stick to these non-lethal drugs. Remember parents, 3 million people a year get addicted to opiates and some within 24 hours. Wouldn't some Tylenol and ice packs (and maybe a little pain) be a better treatment plan for your child's broken arm?

In recent years, it has become a fad for kids to pilfer these medications from their parents' medicine chests to share with their friends. Again, these pills are not party favors. They are dangerous, often addictive medications that can do tremendous harm to your health and well-being. Parents, keep your medications locked up. And kids, if you are offered pills by your friends, decline. It is that simple.

Yes, it can be difficult to say no. Yes, you want to fit in. But at what cost? You are not invincible, and you may just be one of the millions of people predisposed to become addicted. Ask yourself: Is it worth it?

Although not nearly as publicized as opiates, drugs called benzodiazepines, also known as benzos, can be extremely addictive and deadly, as well. People who use benzos describe the resulting feeling as being very similar to the effect of drinking alcohol. I was once given a prescription for a benzo, which I was supposed to take whenever I felt "anxious." Funny thing was, when I took those pills I didn't need to drink—because I felt like I'd already been drinking. Giving an alcoholic a pill that makes him feel drunk, and that he can take whenever he wants, is a recipe for disaster. It doesn't help him stop drinking; it only puts him at risk for becoming addicted to the pills, as well.

But it's okay to take a pill from a doctor, isn't it? That's what the disease tells the addict, and what the addict

tells everyone else. The problem is, that same "addict mind" then starts seeking more of the pills than the doctor prescribed, then more and more, until the common progression of addiction takes over.

Ann's Story

My sister's best friend—I'll call her Ann—ran into this tragic situation. Ann had addiction in her genes, and she liked to drink wine. When she was in her late twenties, she began experiencing body pain and believed she had fibromyalgia (a condition characterized by unexplained pain). Initially, she tried to ignore it, thinking that she was young and it would go away.

It didn't, so one day Ann went to the doctor for her fibromyalgia. The doctor recommended some exercises and gave Ann a prescription for the painkiller Vicodin. That seemed logical to her. She'd noticed that her mom, who also had chronic pain, took pills for relief. Unfortunately, what seemed like a perfectly normal solution for the doctor led to a tragic result.

Ann went home and took one of the pills. But, being an addict, she reacted very strongly to it; it gave her a high similar to that received from illegal drugs. Ann's disease was happy with this.

Not surprisingly, a few weeks later she was taking two pills a day instead of one. That made her feel even "better." Now the disease was delighted. It told her that she really did need those extra pills to alleviate her pain.

Six months later, she was taking four pills a day. Her disease was thrilled—but it had a suggestion.

Ann went back to the doctor and got another prescription, this time for something a bit stronger called Percocet. Percocet made her feel even more high.

A few weeks later, she was taking eight pills a day instead of four.

The next time she went back to the doctor, she asked for something stronger still. The doctor was smart enough to say no, but he did give her a year-long prescription for four Percocet pills a day.

Did the disease surrender at that point? No. Ann, convinced that the doctor was wrong and that she needed *eight* pills a day, simply went to another doctor. An hour later, she walked out with a second prescription for four Percocet a day.

It was all so easy. Over the next few months, Ann visited two more doctors and was able to get enough prescriptions to take sixteen pills a day. Her disease was ecstatic.

Over the next five years, Ann took an increasing number of pills, along with wine every day. The disease reassured her: "Doctors gave you these; it must be okay," and "You need these for pain," and "These pills aren't illegal, so it can't be a problem," and "You're not an addict."

When people asked Ann about the pills, she said she was in serious pain and under a doctor's care, and that she was taking only the prescribed dose—and she believed it!

Of course, she was too high (or in too much pain, depending on who you asked) to hold a job. Year after year, her days consisted of staying home and taking pills for her "back pain." In reality, she was nothing more than an addict overcome by the disease. The only difference between her and a heroin addict was that Ann got her drug from a pharmacy, and the junkie gets his from a dealer on the street.

When Ann turned thirty, she noticed that her body was retaining water and that she bruised easily, so she went to see a doctor. He told her that her liver was failing due to drug and alcohol abuse, and if she didn't get a new liver, she would die.

In desperation, Ann asked what would happen if she stopped drinking and using the pills. Would her liver heal? The doctors said that the human liver rarely heals itself. Once the damage is done, it's permanent. Her only hope was a transplant. Ann was able to get on the liver transplant list by lying about her alcoholism and drug abuse (because it is very difficult to get on a transplant list if the organ damage is due to alcohol abuse).

It didn't matter. Six months later, still waiting for a liver, Ann died—with my sister hugging her. She died from legal alcohol and legal medication, not heroin or cocaine or any other street drug. One small visit to a doctor for pain eventually led to her death.

For Addicts, a Drug Is a Drug

That is what is so scary and dangerous about prescription pills today. Many doctors hand them out to anyone who claims to be in pain. Some doctors even knowingly provide pills to addicts in order to make more money! The addict gets hooked on the pills, which are available from thousands of doctors, some on the Internet. These pills are easy to abuse, and they kill. According to a national survey, in 2010 more than 1.5 million young people were treated for prescription drug complications in emergency rooms—mostly due to overdoses of legal pills.

The good news is that you can avoid these pitfalls. There is no reason you ever have to use opiates or benzos; and if there is addiction in your family you never *should* use them because for you, any exposure to these pills can be as dangerous as taking heroin.

Nowadays, when I go to doctors, I tell them I'm a recovering addict and ask them not to prescribe anything addictive. For example, at a recent appointment, when the doctor suggested I take Vicodin after a small surgery, I politely said no and told him I was a recovering addict. We decided Tylenol was a better choice for me. One easy discussion with my doctor prevented what could have been a terrible relapse.

Most doctors are not addiction experts and might miss the signs that my doctor noticed, or might be fooled by an addict's lies.

So, what should you do to avoid becoming another Ann? First, if your doctor prescribes pain pills to you, tell him or her that you are aware of the addictive properties of certain drugs, and that you would like to avoid those drugs. If you have addiction in your family or you are worried that you may have addiction in your family, absolutely share that with your doctor. The doctor will work with you to manage your pain in a responsible way. Second, if you *must* take this sort of medication, your doctor can control the dosage carefully. And third, never, ever take more than what is prescribed. Consuming extra pills is the first warning sign that addiction is taking over your brain.

Back when I was still drinking, I discovered that if I took pills, I didn't have to drink as much. This made my addict brain happy because I could "prove" to myself and others that I wasn't an alcoholic—and still get drunk. What a stupid theory.

The next time I went to my doctor, who had been seeing me for ten years, I asked for more Xanax, and his response possibly saved my life. He said, "No." Instead, he gave me a non-addictive anxiety pill that I could take every morning and would not be able to abuse. I went away defeated, but I took his advice. Two years later, after I finished my time in rehab, the same doctor told me he knew I was an alcoholic and hadn't felt comfortable giving me addictive pills.

I thank him every time I see him, as I easily could have been Ann.

Unfortunately, what my doctor did is rare. Most doctors are not addiction experts and might miss the signs that my doctor noticed, or might be fooled by an addict's lies. Addicts all over the world are skilled at obtaining pills from dozens of different doctors. They invent stories about pain or anxiety and in minutes are given any addictive pill they want. This pill epidemic has spread across the United States and is now so severe that in 2015 more people in this country died from drug overdoses than from car accidents.

Today, prescription drug abuse is probably an even bigger problem than illegal drug use. Why? Simple: addicts can get the same kinds of drugs from a doctor, which means they're often paid for by insurance. On top of that, the addict and his or her family can justify their behavior much more easily if it involves a "pill from the doctor" rather than a drug from a dealer on the street.

One day scientists will invent pain pills that take away the pain, not the person. Pain pills don't have to be addictive. But until the science of pain management catches up with addiction, we all need to be careful.

Thoughts from Lianna

My aunt took pills for many reasons, the main one being that the disease of addiction wanted her to take them. To me, it was obvious she couldn't make good decisions. She was caught up in herself all the time. The pills made her disease happy, but they made her life—and everyone in it—miserable. You should only take pills that are prescribed to you by a doctor, and don't ever overdo it.

Devotional Message

"At first, 'They eat the bread of wickedness and drink the wine of violence.' Then 'The path of the righteous is like the first gleam of dawn, shining ever brighter till the full light of day.'" —Proverbs 4:17–18

16

The Twelve Steps

If you find yourself drawn to using alcohol and drugs, you may try to convince yourself that you are doing so just to fit in. You may tell yourself that all your friends are doing it. And that you can stop whenever you want. But you know that using drugs and alcohol is wrong. Trying to convince yourself that using is OK is equally wrong.

If you find yourself about to get involved with alcohol and drug use, ask yourself why. Yes, it may be peer pressure that is driving you. But why are you vulnerable to peer pressure? What insecurities, unhappiness, or discontent is driving you to indulge in something you know might hurt you? Talk to a trusted adult; get help fixing what might be bothering you. People who are happy in life do not indulge in substance abuse.

There is a price to pay for addiction. Because of it, we lose our connection to family and friends. You may do poorly in school and in athletics. Adults may lose relationships and jobs. Health can deteriorate and diseases can manifest. And once you fall into the abyss of addiction, there is no cure—ever. There is just treatment and, if it works, a daily struggle to stay clean. You will be setting yourself up for a lifetime of living in recovery, of working to maintain stability and a good and productive life.

> What insecurities, unhappiness, or discontent is driving you to indulge in something you know might hurt you?

An addict cannot cure himself or herself. If you allow yourself to go down this path, you will not be able to cure yourself, either.

That's why treatment and rehabilitation centers (often called rehabs) are so important. Just as you sometimes can't fix your car by yourself and need a mechanic, it often takes a team of addiction experts to "fix" an addict.

Recovery centers focus on:

- Safely stopping the person from taking the drugs or alcohol

- Learning what problems in the person's life contribute to the addiction

- Examining family history

- Teaching the addict new, healthy ways to deal with the stress that comes into everyone's life.

The Twelve Steps

The Twelve Steps were developed in the 1930s by the founders of Alcoholics Anonymous and have helped millions of people stop using drugs/alcohol so they can live normal, healthy, happy lives. Addicts often say that stopping the drinking was the easy part, while learning to live peacefully was the hard part. The Twelve Steps help with that, too.

Hopefully, with the help of this book, you will never need the Twelve Steps, but you should read them carefully to better understand the addicts in your life—and what you would face if you succumbed to alcohol or drug addiction. Groups such as Al-Anon (a support group for those whose loved ones are addicts) discuss this in much more detail.

Here are the steps. In Alcoholics Anonymous we:

1. Admitted we were powerless over alcohol—that our lives had become unmanageable.

2. Came to believe that a Power greater than ourselves could restore us to sanity.

3. Made a decision to turn our will and our lives over to the care of God as we understood Him.

4. Made a searching and fearless moral inventory of ourselves.

5. Admitted to God, to ourselves, and to another human being the exact nature of our wrongs.

6. Were entirely ready to have God remove all these defects of character.

7. Humbly asked Him to remove our shortcomings.

8. Made a list of all persons we had harmed, and became willing to make amends to them all.

9. Made direct amends to such people wherever possible, except when to do so would injure them or others.

10. Continued to take personal inventory and when we were wrong promptly admitted it.

11. Sought through prayer and meditation to improve our conscious contact with God as we understood Him, praying only for knowledge of His will for us and the power to carry that out.

12. Having had a spiritual awakening as the result of these steps, we tried to carry this message to alcoholics and to practice these principles in all our affairs.

The Twelve Steps are an important aspect of thousands of recovery programs around the world and have helped millions of people find sobriety and peace. True recovery is about more than no longer drinking alcohol or taking drugs. For addicts, "recovering" means learning to live happily and peacefully, without having to use drugs and alcohol to deal with life. Addicts call this "living life on life's terms."

The Promises

The goal of true recovery is best summarized in the Promises of Alcoholics Anonymous. These oaths describe what recovering addicts are certain to find in sobriety with the help of AA. You may notice that the Promises deal more with how addicts can live their lives normally and happily than with drugs and alcohol. Many people think drugs and alcohol are the only issue with addicts, but that's not so.

Addicts use drugs to cope with life's ups and downs, so they never really develop the coping skills that non-addicts have. That is, they don't know how to handle setbacks and stress in a healthy way. Thus, the Promises are what a true recovery program helps addicts attain:

- If we are painstaking about this phase of our development, we will be amazed before we are halfway through.

- We are going to know a new freedom and a new happiness.

- We will not regret the past nor wish to shut the door on it.

- We will comprehend the word *serenity* and we will know peace.

- No matter how far down the scale we have gone, we will see how our experience can benefit others.

- That feeling of uselessness and self-pity will disappear.

- We will lose interest in selfish things and gain interest in our fellows.

- Self-seeking will slip away.

- Our whole attitude and outlook upon life will change.

- Fear of people and of economic insecurity will leave us.

- We will intuitively know how to handle situations that used to baffle us.

- We will suddenly realize that God is doing for us what we could not do for ourselves.

- Are these extravagant promises? We think not.

- They are being fulfilled among us—sometimes quickly, sometimes slowly.

- They will always materialize if we work for them.

When I finally got desperate enough to go to rehab, I had no idea I would be taught anything more than how to quit drinking or helped beyond making sure I safely stopped. It turned out that, for me, not drinking was the *easy* part of rehab. With dozens of experts and fellow addicts around me, not drinking for a few days was simple. But I soon began to realize that rehabilitation and sobriety are really about learning new coping skills and how to live a joyous, happy, free life.

During my years of active alcoholism, I had only one coping skill: whether I was stressed, sick, mad, scared, anxious, alone, or even excited, I drank. Developing healthy coping skills to deal with these emotions is what sobriety is really about. When I first read the Promises, I thought they were crazy and impossible to attain. But they have all come true for me, as they have for millions of addicts.

Thoughts from Lianna

In class, I learned about Indian religions. In Buddhism, there is a path to "enlightenment." That's when you feel full of peace instead of suffering and longing for things all the time. Buddhists call it the Eightfold Path. I look at the Twelve Steps like the Eightfold Path. To get to enlightenment in addiction, you have to follow the steps to help make you better.

Devotional Message

"'Follow me,' Jesus said to him, and Levi got up, left everything and followed him." —Luke 5:27b–28

If your family member has stopped using drugs, that means he or she is like Levi: he or she left the drugs and followed Jesus's call to stop.

17

I Can Decide MY Future

Throughout this book, you have learned that although you may have been born with the genes to become an addict, you also have the power to prevent those genes from becoming active. You have also learned that even those who do not have addiction in their families can be susceptible to it, and that many people have it in their genes and do not know it. Most diseases do not provide us with a clear opportunity to avoid them. A woman with the predilection for breast cancer in her genes can't prevent the disease from forming. No known cure is available for genetic diabetes. People born into families with problem hearts can exercise and eat healthily, yet heart attacks still occur. But you, by controlling your behavior and what goes into your body, can keep the disease of addiction asleep forever.

This chapter will give you some easy-to-remember rules to help you lead a life free of addiction. They aren't magic wands, and they aren't the Big Answers to All Your Questions. In the world of addiction, even doctors do not have all the answers; there's still plenty that no one knows. If you have other resources in your life that provide information about addiction, by all means listen to them, as well.

We'll start with the important question: "Can I ever use drugs or alcohol?" Here are our "nonscientific" suggestions.

Illegal Drugs

The rule for this one is easy: never. *Never, ever use illegal drugs.* Simple to remember, isn't it? I can't tell you how many addicts I have spoken with who became addicted the first time they tried cocaine, heroin, or another illegal drug. Yes, the *very first time.* So, what might be considered "experimenting" with drugs for some kids could be a horrible mistake for you.

Fortunately, our government helps you with this decision by labeling some drugs as illegal. The fear of going to prison is enough to help some people stay away from such drugs—but for you, this should be only a starting point. The threat of rousing the disease of addiction should be the main thing that makes you afraid of using illegal narcotics.

Remember, these drugs are not labeled "illegal" by accident. They are very dangerous to *anyone* using them. In fact, many people die the first time they use such drugs. Cocaine kills thousands of first-time users each year. Heroin sends thousands of people to hospitals for overdoses the first time they try it.

Not only are illegal drugs dangerous in and of themselves, they are often laced with harmful substances. Lacing is the adding of one or more substances to another in order to bulk up the original substance. This is done for a lot of different reasons, but the most common reason is to be able to make more money. When a dealer laces a drug with a substance that is effective but cheaper, more money is made.

Unfortunately, the health and well-being of users is not at the forefront of the minds of drug dealers. Thus, drugs are often laced with chemicals that are even more harmful than the drugs themselves. It is not uncommon for drugs to be adulterated with poisons like strychnine, formaldehyde, and even gasoline, consumption of which can be lethal in and of itself.

So, for illegal drugs, remember the simple rule: *never.* They are illegal and very dangerous to everyone. To a potential addict, a single use might switch on the addiction gene forever. To any user, the chemicals with which these drugs are often laced may be fatal.

Prescription Drugs

The rule is: always follow your doctor's instructions. As discussed earlier in this book, there are dozens of drugs that a doctor can prescribe that are extremely addictive and especially dangerous to an addict. If the addiction gene has already been turned on, the addict should stay away from such pills unless they are absolutely necessary.

Of course, in certain situations strong pain pills might be essential. One recovering addict I know had to have back surgery—the kind of surgery where a Tylenol or aspirin is not enough to combat the pain. Because this person is 100 percent dedicated to his sobriety, he took extraordinary steps to make sure he did not abuse the pills: he had a friend keep them, and bring him one every eight hours—just as the doctor prescribed.

My friend did the right thing. He needed these strong pills for genuine pain, but he made sure he could not abuse them. This leads us back to our simple rule for prescription pills: *always take the medicine exactly as prescribed by your doctor*. Don't take a pill an hour early and tell yourself you had to, because your doctor doesn't understand you. Don't take two pills instead of one because it's easier. Just follow the doctor's orders *exactly*.

A second rule to remember: inform your doctor about your family history. Telling the doctor that you have addiction in your family tree will be a huge help for your future. Don't be embarrassed. Remember, addiction is a disease, and there's no shame in that.

Alcohol

Do you really have to go your entire life without ever having a drink of alcohol? Is it even possible? When your parents throw a dinner party, how much wine or beer is around? When you go to a football game, isn't beer everywhere? How about weddings—have you ever noticed how many people drink at weddings?

Still, the rule is definite: if you have addiction in your family, *never drink alcohol*. That's the safest way to avoid turning on the addiction gene. Remember, billions of people in the world live this way. Just stay away from alcohol in any form. And if you don't know if you have addiction in your family, take the safe route and assume you do.

You might think that's ridiculous. Surely you can have one little drink now and then. Well, the problem is that it's not clear how much alcohol is required to turn on the addiction gene. Four years of daily drinking in college? One glass of wine at a wedding? Even the experts don't know. For Josh Hamilton, his very first drink might have turned on his disease. For me, it took years.

No one else, not even your parents, can control your choices and your future the way you can.

Where does that leave *you*? Again, the easy number to remember is *zero*. Zero drinks will ensure that you never become an active alcoholic.

Let's revisit our list:

- Illegal drugs: *never*.

- Legal drugs: *take exactly as ordered by the doctor* (and tell your doctor about any family history of addiction).

- Alcohol: *stay away.*

In the 1980s, when drug abuse was growing into a real problem for teenagers and others in the United States, the president's wife, Nancy Reagan, came out with a program entitled "Just Say No to Drugs." While this might have been a good idea, it was not enough for kids with and without addiction in their family. Telling young people that drugs are dangerous was not enough incentive, as we can tell by the fact that in the thirty years since, addiction rates have gone up, not down.

If you are someone with addiction in your family, what you need to know is that while "Just Say No to Drugs" might be possible for other kids, for you the message needs to be something like "Just Say No to *All* Drugs— Don't Consider Experimenting with Them, Not Even Once, or You Might Ruin the Rest of Your Life. *Danger!*"

The same thing is true of alcohol. Stay away from it, even on the occasions when everyone around *you* is drinking (like a toast of champagne at a wedding). Remember, addicts can't ever drink like "normal" people. The disease makes us different.

Thoughts from Lianna

This section is my personal favorite. It teaches you that you *do* have a say. It's your life, you know! Your parent might decide to drink or do drugs, but you can decide not to. You know that drugs and drinking aren't the right things to do with your life. I believe in you, and that you will make the right decision.

No one else, not even your parents, can control your choices and your future the way you can. Do you want to make the most of your life? I know I do! I believe in free will and that every person has a conscience, so use yours!

Your life is precious. Your future is so important I can't even begin to explain it. Do yourself a favor and never do drugs; it is an easy decision.

Right now, I'm on a competitive soccer team. I play defender. Okay, I know what you're thinking: why are you talking about soccer in this book? Well, here's the thing. My coach teaches me never to give up, and to protect the goal. Your goal should be never to do drugs. You can protect the goal by protecting yourself from exposure to all drugs, all alcohol, all forms of addiction. If you never give up on your goal in life, you'll score a win!

18

The Peanut vs. The Potato

Whether you know you have addiction in your genes or not, you now understand that addiction is a disease that cannot be cured but can be prevented. We've armed you with knowledge about the disease and ways to avoid it. We've also given you tips to support you when things get difficult. Now, I want to talk to you about peanuts and potatoes.

Yep, peanuts and potatoes.

Most of us know people who have a peanut allergy. They cannot eat peanuts, or any food with peanuts in it, without a severe physical reaction. This is where the "peanut" comes in; it represents a food allergy.

The potato? Simple: vodka is a type of alcohol made from potatoes, so we're using potatoes to represent alcohol and drugs.

Peanuts versus potatoes. You see?

Some children's peanut allergies are so strong that, when they're at school, no one else in their entire *class* can bring peanuts. These kids have such a severe allergic reaction that not only they but everyone around them must always be aware of it, to keep them from eating peanuts. Teachers will even notify the parents of all the other students in class about a kid's peanut allergy.

Most airlines hand out peanuts for a snack, but when the airline is alerted that someone on board has a peanut allergy, they will not serve peanuts to anyone on that plane because the allergy can be so dangerous.

People treat peanut allergies this seriously because if a person with the allergy is exposed to peanuts, that person might die.

Does this sound familiar?

You might know other people with egg allergies, milk allergies, or chocolate allergies, not to mention any of the hundreds of allergies that have nothing to do with food. What do these kids and their families do about the allergy? Simple: at all costs, they avoid the item or items that trigger the reaction.

What does this mean for you? Remember, the first chapter of this book explained that most doctors believe addiction is similar to an allergy. Just as someone who has a peanut allergy is born with it, most addicts are born "allergic" to alcohol and drugs.

Unfortunately, anyone can have a "potato" allergy. Equally unfortunately, our society doesn't prepare kids to deal with the addiction allergy. Unlike your "peanut" friend, other people in your class don't know about your "potato" allergy. You aren't told to avoid the things that trigger your illness when you go to parties or football games, or sit on a plane next to someone consuming your allergic substance.

Addiction is a disease. It should be talked about rather than ignored; it's not something to be ashamed of.

Think about that. Is the "potato" (alcohol and drugs) any different for you than peanuts are for your allergic friend? No. You're allergic to the potato, and your friend is allergic to the peanut. Unfortunately, while our society is very open about the peanut allergy, we rarely talk about the potato allergy. In order for children of addiction to survive, this needs to change.

Peanut allergies need to be recognized and acknowledged by teachers, classmates, parents, and society. And so does the predisposition to addiction to the potato. The difference in these allergies is that the peanut allergy creates an immediate reaction while the potato allergy may take a bit longer to seem to activate. But these allergies do have a lot in common:

- Sometimes an allergy, any allergy, can take a while to show itself. You may eat peanuts or shellfish five times before you have an allergic reaction. You may drink or do drugs several times before addiction kicks in. But an allergy is an allergy, and once it goes live, it does not go away.

- People with peanut allergies can avoid a terrible reaction by never eating peanuts. The same goes for people allergic to potatoes.

- Kids with peanut allergies should not hang around kids eating peanuts. Same with the potato.

- Kids with peanut allergies shouldn't sit on a plane next to someone eating peanuts. You shouldn't hang out with someone drinking the potato.

- Families of people with peanut allergies always know about the problem and make sure to keep peanuts away from their loved ones. They should do the same for those of us who suffer from "potato" allergies!

- Families with peanut allergies are careful about peanut allergies developing in other family members. They recognize that peanut allergies can be passed down from generation to generation. Families with potato allergies should recognize the same thing.

Your friend with the peanut allergy learned to live a normal and happy life without eating peanuts until doing so became second nature. He knows he's allergic to peanuts, that eating peanuts could be deadly for him, so he takes precautions never to eat peanuts—and he's not ashamed of any of it.

Your allergy—or potential allergy—is no different! You're allergic to alcohol and drugs instead of peanuts, that's all. And you can live without them. Avoiding the "potato" will eventually become second nature to you.

Still, you, your family, and your friends must first acknowledge that the allergy exists, and then work together to keep you away from drugs and alcohol. That way, you can become one of the billions of people who have never used alcohol or drugs—and who live full, normal, happy lives.

Addiction is a disease. It should be talked about rather than ignored; it's not something to be ashamed of. Does anyone hide his or her peanut allergy? No, that would be silly, not to mention dangerous. Do families discuss and acknowledge their peanut allergies? Yes. But families don't normally discuss and acknowledge their "potato" allergies, even though this failure is just as silly and dangerous as ignoring a peanut allergy is.

When I was a child, my sister and I were told about our numerous allergies to food, but I wasn't warned that I might be allergic to alcohol. Nor was my sister, who is six years sober as I write this (and inspiring others as a speaker at AA meetings and mental illness support groups such as the National Alliance for Mental Illness), told that she had an allergy to drugs.

My food allergy is to shellfish. From an early age, I was constantly reminded that I was allergic to shrimp, lobster—any seafood in a shell. I was warned that I must avoid these foods forever. What happened? Well, I *have* avoided these foods my whole life. It hasn't even been hard: I just make sure people know about my allergy and that dishes at restaurants don't contain shellfish. Easy.

But although I've known about my shellfish allergy for forty years, I became aware of my alcohol allergy only eight years ago. If I'd known about that allergy all along, would I have been able to avoid activating it? Maybe. At least I would have had a fighting chance. But sadly, I was encouraged to drink instead.

I'm now aware that I have a severe allergy to alcohol. My kids are aware that they're likely to have the same allergic reaction to alcohol or drugs . . . and that that reaction lasts a lifetime and affects everything and everyone in their future.

With the information you have learned from this book, you can change this situation for yourself and your family. Just ask yourself this question: "With so much to lose, and nothing to gain, why even start using drugs or alcohol?"

I finished this book at 8 a.m. on a school day. And the day has already been amazing. I was up at 5:30 a.m. to play with our puppy and wake my daughter up to get ready for school. In the next hour, I was able to feed the kids (and the puppy), say I love you and goodbye to my wife and son, and drive my daughter thirty-five minutes to her new school. Those thirty-five minutes were truly magnificent—filled with peace, love, humor, and joy. We joked about boys, sports, bad drivers, politics . . . and, of course, she took over my radio with her music.

Upon arrival she said, "I love you, Daddy," shut the door, and walked up the stairs. I smiled, paused to enjoy the moment, and finally drove off as a proud father who was able to be part of her day.

Today I did not sleep through my children's lives. Today I was not hung over. Today I was not an absent father. Today I was at peace.

Today was a good day.

Study Guide

Chapter 1

Vocabulary

For each vocabulary word listed below:

- Find the sentence in which it is used in the chapter.

- Define the word as it is used in the sentence.

- Tell what part of speech the word is used as in the sentence.

Excess, Addiction, Predisposition, Genetic, Prevalence, Status

Questions

1. As you respond to each of the following questions, cite and use examples from the chapter.

2. How is a predisposition toward substance abuse passed down by family members?

3. What does our author, Marc, wish he had known when he was a preteen? Why?

4. What is the purpose of this book? What is its one goal?

5. How are alcoholism and addiction alike?

Chapter 2

Vocabulary

For each vocabulary word listed below:

- Find the sentence in which it is used in the chapter.
- Define the word as it is used in the sentence.
- Tell what part of speech the word is used as in the sentence.

Activate, Inherited, Narcotics, DNA, Environment, Rehabilitate, Propensity

Questions

1. Can addiction ever be cured? Why?

2. What part of the body is responsible for addiction? Explain.

3. What factors other than predisposition can lead someone to become an addict?

Chapter 3

Vocabulary

For each vocabulary word listed below:

- Find the sentence in which it is used in the chapter.
- Define the word as it is used in the sentence.
- Tell what part of speech the word is used as in the sentence.

Conceal, Transfer, Siblings, Devastate, Intentionally, Deliberately, Potential

Questions

1. How is someone with a predisposition towards addiction different from others?

2. Can you ever know with certainty whether or not you have a predisposition to addiction?

3. How do we define an addict?

4. Name three ways addiction can change your life.

Chapter 4

Vocabulary

For each vocabulary word listed below:

- Find the sentence in which it is used in the chapter.

- Define the word as it is used in the sentence.

- Tell what part of speech the word is used as in the sentence.

- Find the sentence in the chapter in which each of the following words is used, and then define the word as it is used in that sentence. Also include the part of speech as which it is used.

Bizarre, Glorify, Inherent, Recreational, Environment, Optimal,

Questions

1. Why are addict families less likely to discuss serious issues than non-addict families?

1. What role might a person's environment play in whether or not they use alcohol or drugs?

1. What is an optimal age for kids to begin discussing substance abuse? Why?

1. What are two signs there might be substance abuse in a family?

Chapter 5

Vocabulary

For each vocabulary word listed below:

- Find the sentence in which it is used in the chapter.

- Define the word as it is used in the sentence.

- Tell what part of speech the word is used as in the sentence.

Progressive, Adaptive, Neglect, Consumption, Hindsight, Fraternity, Justification, Willpower

Questions

1. How many stages of addiction are there? What are they?

2. During the first stage of addiction, why might someone use alcohol or drugs?

3. What are three things that often happen to people in the conclusion stage of addiction?

4. What does the phrase "Hindsight is 20/20 vision" mean? Think of an instance in your life to which you might apply this phrase.

Chapter 6

Vocabulary

For each vocabulary word listed below:

- Find the sentence in which it is used in the chapter.

- Define the word as it is used in the sentence.

- Tell what part of speech the word is used as in the sentence.

Majority, Concern, Plight, Distress

Questions

1. What are feelings?

2. What are some of the feelings you have when you think about or see someone who is an alcoholic or an addict?

3. What are your feelings about alcohol and drugs?

Chapter 7

Vocabulary

For each vocabulary word listed below:

- Find the sentence in which it is used in the chapter.

- Define the word as it is used in the sentence.

- Tell what part of speech the word is used as in the sentence.

Convince, Persuade, Anxiety, Dissipate

Questions

1. What are some of the diseases associated with prolonged or careless substance abuse?

2. What trick does addiction play on an addict that makes it difficult to overcome?

Chapter 8

Vocabulary

For each vocabulary word listed below:

- Find the sentence in which it is used in the chapter.
- Define the word as it is used in the sentence.
- Tell what part of speech the word is used as in the sentence.

Genetics, Empowers, Irrational, Succumb

Questions
1. What are some ways in which we may be genetically similar to our parents?
2. Name two ways in which our environment might make us similar to our parents.
3. Which do you think is a stronger influence on us, genetics or environment? Why?

Chapter 9

Vocabulary

For each vocabulary word listed below:

- Find the sentence in which it is used in the chapter.

- Define the word as it is used in the sentence.

- Tell what part of speech the word is used as in the sentence.

Deliberately, Controversy, Relapse, Denial, Cycle

Questions

1. What is one of the basic principles of recovery for addicts? What does this tell you about drugs and alcohol?

2. Who, besides an addict, might be in denial about the addict's disease? Why might they be in denial?

3. What is the impact of denial on addiction?

Chapter 10

Vocabulary

For each vocabulary word listed below:

- Find the sentence in which it is used in the chapter.

- Define the word as it is used in the sentence.

- Tell what part of speech the word is used as in the sentence.

Avoid, Temptation, Peer pressure, Unconditionally, Resolving, Ultimately

Questions

1. If you are dealing with peer pressure to use drugs or alcohol, with whom might you share your anxiety about it? To whom should you turn for advice?

2. Discuss a time you experienced peer pressure, how it made you feel, and how you responded to it. Are you pleased with your response? If not, to whom could you have turned for help?

Chapter 11

Vocabulary

For each vocabulary word listed below:

- Find the sentence in which it is used in the chapter.

- Define the word as it is used in the sentence.

- Tell what part of speech the word is used as in the sentence.

Coerced, Pranking, Reluctant, Potential

Questions

1. Why is it OK for you to say you're allergic to drugs and alcohol even if your parents are not alcoholics?

2. What is the "No, Go, Tell" rule?

3. Why might you be reluctant to use this rule? What are the benefits of using it?

Chapter 12

Vocabulary

For each vocabulary word listed below:

- Find the sentence in which it is used in the chapter.

- Define the word as it is used in the sentence.

- Tell what part of speech the word is used as in the sentence.

Notable, Illicit, Functions, Respected, Sober

Questions

1. Why might we pressure ourselves to do things we know are not in our best interest?

2. What are some things you can do with friends other than experiment with alcohol or drugs?

3. What should you do if all your friends seem interested in, is experimenting with alcohol or drugs?

Chapter 13

Vocabulary

For each vocabulary word listed below:

- Find the sentence in which it is used in the chapter.

- Define the word as it is used in the sentence.

- Tell what part of speech the word is used as in the sentence.

Inoculations, Dormant, Despair

Questions

1. According to experts, is there any real cure for addiction? Why?

2. What is the best means of avoiding addiction? What are some of the difficulties involved in doing so?

3. What does the author mean when he says, "Knowledge is power"?

Chapter 14

Vocabulary

For each vocabulary word listed below:

- Find the sentence in which it is used in the chapter.

- Define the word as it is used in the sentence.

- Tell what part of speech the word is used as in the sentence.

Formation, Potions, Rehabilitation, Jeopardy

Questions

1. What are the two principles of Alcoholics Anonymous and Narcotics Anonymous that seem to make them work?

2. Before Alcoholics Anonymous, what were some of the cures for addiction suggested by doctors and experts?

3. What do you think Lianna means when she says, "You should not be afraid to do something about your situation"? Give an example of how Lianna's advice might apply in your life.

Chapter 15

Vocabulary

For each vocabulary word listed below:

- Find the sentence in which it is used in the chapter.

- Define the word as it is used in the sentence.

- Tell what part of speech the word is used as in the sentence.

Opiates, Epidemic, Overdose, Initial, Ravaging, Complex, Advocate, Ecstatic

Questions

1. Why are opiates in such widespread use? Why are they dangerous?

2. Is it always OK to take pills prescribed by a doctor? When might it not be?

3. What should you do if a doctor prescribes you opiates for pain? Why?

Chapter 16

Vocabulary

For each vocabulary word listed below:

- Find the sentence in which it is used in the chapter.

- Define the word as it is used in the sentence.

- Tell what part of speech the word is used as in the sentence.

Discontent, Inventory, Humbly, Meditation, Intuitively, Enlightenment

Questions

1. What is the price we pay for addiction?

2. With what do addicts use drugs and alcohol to cope?

3. What are some of the stressors in your life? How do you cope with them?

Chapter 17

Vocabulary

For each vocabulary word listed below:

- Find the sentence in which it is used in the chapter.

- Define the word as it is used in the sentence.

- Tell what part of speech the word is used as in the sentence.

Adulterated, Predilection

Questions

1. List the rules that will help you lead a life free from addiction. What would you add to this?

2. What character traits do you need to stay substance-free? How can you nurture those qualities in yourself?

3. What was the most important lesson you learned from reading this book?

ABOUT THE AUTHORS

Lianna is a busy teen. When she's not on Instagram or Snap Chatting and Face Timing her friends, she's diligently studying and playing high school sports like soccer, softball, and field hockey. Her favorite school activity is serving as an officer on the ASBC (Associated Student Body Council). In her spare time, she volunteers for local charities and raises money for Rady Children's Hospital. In fact, she loves kids so much she wants to be a pediatrician. Lianna attends one of the top high schools in California, and is enjoying the challenges she faces there and the friends she has made.

Marc enjoys spending time with his family and their new Yorkie puppy, Coco. He is an executive of a utility company, which keeps him very busy and allows him to travel throughout the country. When Marc isn't working or on his phone, his hobbies include: embarrassing his wife and kids, convincing his daughter that boys are bad, passing his musical tastes to his son, cleaning-up puppy pee inside the house, and talking politics to anyone that will listen.

Rowena is a stay-at-home mom who is dedicated to raising her two children and serving her community through philanthropy. When she's not driving the kids around to all their activities, she spends her time volunteering at school, raising money for Rady Children's Hospital and working for local non-profits through the National Charity League. When she's not trying to save the world, she enjoys traveling, eating out, watching movies, attending concerts and finding peace at the spa.

Bennett is a typical teenage boy. His favorite hobbies are playing Air Soft and video games, watching/filming YouTube videos, listening to his tunes, and participating in sports like soccer, basketball, and track & field. He also has a black belt in Tae Kwon Do. His favorite school subjects are history and math. Although he loves his dog, he has a pretty serious collection of pigs, his favorite animal. If stranded on a deserted island, he could survive on rice, chicken wings, and chocolate.

CPSIA information can be obtained
at www.ICGtesting.com
Printed in the USA
FSHW04n1544040418
46522FS

9 780997 426328